IMMERSION
Bible Studies

MICAH
NAHUM
HABAKKUK
ZEPHANIAH
HAGGAI
ZECHARIAH
MALACHI

Praise for IMMERSION

"IMMERSION BIBLE STUDIES is a powerful tool in helping readers to hear God speak through Scripture and to experience a deeper faith as a result."
Adam Hamilton, author of *24 Hours That Changed the World*

"I highly commend to you IMMERSION BIBLE STUDIES, which tells us what the Bible teaches and how to apply it personally."
John Ed Mathison, author of *Treasures of the Transformed Life*

"If you're looking for a deeper knowledge and understanding of God's Word, you must dive into IMMERSION BIBLE STUDIES. Whether in a group setting or as an individual, you will experience God and his unconditional love for each of us in a whole new way."
Pete Wilson, founding and senior pastor of Cross Point Church

"This beautiful series helps readers become fluent in the words and thoughts of God, for purposes of illumination, strength building, and developing a closer walk with the One who loves us so."
Laurie Beth Jones, author of *Jesus, CEO* and *The Path*

"The IMMERSION BIBLE STUDIES series is no less than a game changer. It ignites the purpose and power of Scripture by showing us how to do more than just know God or love God; it gives us the tools to love like God as well."
Shane Stanford, author of *You Can't Do Everything . . . So Do Something*

IMMERSION
Bible Studies

MICAH, NAHUM, HABAKKUK, ZEPHANIAH, HAGGAI, ZECHARIAH, MALACHI

Linda B. Hinton

Abingdon Press

Nashville

MICAH, NAHUM, HABAKKUK, ZEPHANIAH,
HAGGAI, ZECHARIAH, MALACHI
IMMERSION BIBLE STUDIES
by Linda B. Hinton

Library of Congress Cataloging-in-Publication Data
Hinton, Linda B.
  Micah, Nahum, Habakkuk, Zephaniah, Haggai, Zechariah, Malachi / Linda B. Hinton.
    pages cm. — (Immersion Bible studies)
  ISBN 978-1-4267-1640-9 (book - pbk. unsewn/adhesive bound : alk. paper) 1. Bible.
Minor Prophets—Textbooks. I. Title.
  BS1560.H45 2013
  224'.906—dc23
                                                                            2013016737

Editor: Jan Turrentine
Leader Guide Writer: Jan Turrentine

13 14 15 16 17 18 19 20 21 22—10 9 8 7 6 5 4 3 2 1

Manufactured in the United States of America

Contents

Review Team

Diane Blum
Pastor and Spiritual Director
Nashville, Tennessee

Susan Cox
Pastor
McMurry United Methodist Church
Claycomo, Missouri

Margaret Ann Crain
Professor of Christian Education
Garrett-Evangelical Theological Seminary
Evanston, Illinois

Nan Duerling
Curriculum Writer and Editor
Cambridge, Maryland

Paul Escamilla
Pastor and Writer
St. John's United Methodist Church
Austin, Texas

James Hawkins
Pastor and Writer
Smyrna, Delaware

Andrew Johnson
Professor of New Testament
Nazarene Theological Seminary
Kansas City, Missouri

Snehlata Patel
Pastor
Woodrow United Methodist Church
Staten Island, New York

Emerson B. Powery
Professor of New Testament
Messiah College
Grantham, Pennsylvania

Clayton Smith
Pastoral Staff
Church of the Resurrection
Leawood, Kansas

Harold Washington
Professor of Hebrew Bible
Saint Paul School of Theology
Kansas City, Missouri

Carol Wehrheim
Curriculum Writer and Editor
Princeton, New Jersey

Immersion Bible Studies

A fresh new look at the Bible, from beginning to end,
and what it means in your life.

Welcome to Immersion!

We've asked some of the leading Bible scholars, teachers, and pastors to help us with a new kind of Bible study. Immersion remains true to Scripture but always asks, "Where are you in your life? What do you struggle with? What makes you rejoice?" Then it helps you read the Scriptures to discover their deep, abiding truths. Immersion is about God and God's Word, and it is also about you—not just your thoughts, but your feelings and your faith.

In each study you will prayerfully read the Scripture and reflect on it. Then you will engage it in three ways:

Claim Your Story
> Through stories and questions, think about your life, with its struggles and joys.

Enter the Bible Story
> Explore Scripture and consider what God is saying to you.

Live the Story
> Reflect on what you have discovered, and put it into practice in your life.

IMMERSION makes use of an exciting new translation of Scripture, the Common English Bible (CEB). The CEB and IMMERSION BIBLE STUDIES will offer adults:

- the emotional expectation to find the love of God
- the rational expectation to find the knowledge of God
- reliable, genuine, and credible power to transform lives
- clarity of language

Whether you are using the Common English Bible or another translation, IMMERSION BIBLE STUDIES will offer a refreshing plunge into God's Word, your life, and your life with God.

1.

The Minor Prophets: Noise, Light, and Hope

Micah—Malachi

Claim Your Story

Global Positioning System (GPS) devices are great tools. They can show you where you are and what's ahead, behind, and to the side. They even talk! The information you get from them, however, is only as good as what's in them. On a recent trip, my GPS was on target most of the way. Unfortunately, close to the destination, it ran out of information. The map had not been updated, and while I was seeing streets and houses in front of me, the GPS showed only blank space.

Scripture can function like a GPS device for our lives, providing guidance as we navigate day-to-day life. Bible study keeps our scriptural GPS up to date, but sometimes it's hard to understand what we are reading and how it can help. Does Scripture seem like a blank to you, with nothing that applies to your situation? Or is there so much information that you get confused and disoriented, not sure where to turn?

The Minor Prophets of the Old Testament can present some challenges in these ways. Their combined ministries cover over two hundred years of complex history. Their words are often forceful, blunt, and confrontational. Some of the violent imagery can make us wince and want to turn away. Their visions and dreams may seem too far removed from reality to be useful.

So, what is in their stories for us to claim as our story? First, they tell us what God is like. We see what God does and what God says in the very bad times as well as in the good times for God's people. Knowing and understanding God better is the first priority.

Next, we are told explicitly what God expects of us and the consequences of disobedience. The Minor Prophets tell us over and over again that God is committed to revealing God's will for us and for the world. Each prophet also tells us that there is hope, always hope.

They show us what it's like to answer God's call even when it's hard and to trust God even when the next step isn't clear. They have much to teach us about our own hard calls and uncertainty about our own next steps.

Enter the Bible Story

Called for Hard Times

God tends to call prophets for hard times. Prophets don't usually show up just to tell us that we're doing great. They rebuke, challenge, guide, and hold up a not-so-comfortable mirror in which we see ourselves. Prophets offer us a chance to update our internal GPS, to find our spiritual road map, and to get back on the road to our true destination. They do offer hope and reassurance, but there's some harsh truth to face in the meantime. The Minor Prophets were called for such times.

They were faithful, obedient, and passionate, sometimes angry or even fearful. They were stubborn and stood their ground when people did not like what they said. They held onto their mission to tell the truth so that those receiving their messages could live a better life full of righteousness and blessing.

Their books are labeled "minor" not because their messages are less important than others, but because of their length in relation to other prophets such as Isaiah and Jeremiah. The Minor Prophets are sometimes referred to as the Latter Prophets because of their place at the end of the Old Testament era and Old Testament Scriptures. The Minor Prophets are also grouped with five other prophetic books to make up the Book of the Twelve: Hosea, Joel, Amos, Obadiah, Jonah, Micah, Nahum,

Habakkuk, Zephaniah, Haggai, Zechariah, and Malachi. These prophets had many of the same concerns and messages as the Major Prophets. They all confronted the community of faith with their lack of respect for God, their moral and ethical failures, their tolerance of polluted worship, and the horrendous consequences of their sin.

The ministries of many of these prophets, both major and minor, overlap one another. Beginning in the mid-eighth century B.C., they worked and spoke for over two hundred years during some of the most turbulent times that God's people ever faced. When the first ones answered God's call to prophesy, Israel and Judah were independent nations. By the end, the state of Israel was no more, and Judah was controlled by foreigners.

We are not told much about these men who were called by God to be God's spokesmen. Some, like Zephaniah, were prominent in their community. He was a descendant of King Hezekiah of Judah. Zechariah was connected to the Temple and may have been a priest. Many prophets, however, were like Micah, who was called from his ordinary life in a small village to enter the larger arena of prophecy and power. The Minor Prophets' importance lies in their willingness to be at God's disposal. They heard, saw, and spoke both the hard and the soft words to their people on God's behalf.

The Minor Prophets lived through sad and dangerous days, and they shared the suffering of their people. As God's messengers, the prophets helped the community of faith move from being a political and military power to living more as a spiritual force in the world. By the time of Malachi, the Israelites no longer had complete control of their government, but they still had the covenant. They still had God's promises and God's presence, whether they lived in Judah or never returned from exile.

Called to Speak

"In the beginning," God spoke the created order into existence. God was also straightforward in his expectations for humankind and about the consequences of disobedience. We are to take care of our world on God's behalf, live in harmony with one another and with God, and respect the limits God puts on our lives (Genesis 1–3).

About the Scripture

Prophecy for Troubled Times

While there is scholarly disagreement over some of the exact dates for the Minor Prophets, we can see that the Israelites (in Israel, Judah, and in exile) had abundant prophetic leadership for these trying times.

Jonah	c. 786–746 B.C.
Amos	c. 760–750 B.C.
Isaiah 1–39	c. 750–700 B.C.
Micah	c. 736-687 B.C.
State of Israel absorbed by Assyria	*724 B.C.*
Zephaniah	c. 640–609 B.C.
Nahum	c. 626–612 B.C.
Habakkuk	c. 626–612 B.C.
Jeremiah	c. 627–572 B.C.
Jerusalem captured by Babylonia, Exile begins	*597 B.C.*
Ezekiel	c. 593–571 B.C.
Jerusalem destroyed by Babylonia	*587 B.C.*
Isaiah 40–55	539 B.C.
Judah controlled by Persia	*539 B.C.*
Exiles allowed to return to Judah, rebuild the Temple	*539 B.C.*
Isaiah 56–66	c. 530–510 B.C.
Haggai	c. 520 B.C.
Zechariah	c. 520–518 B.C.
Malachi	c. 515–445 B.C.

The prophetic word is also straightforward. It always rests on what God says at Creation and on God's instructions to his people since then. It grows out of the long relationship between God and the chosen people, out of their history together in all the big events and small details. The prophetic word rests on Law, covenant, and God's faithfulness.

What the prophets say is backed by the creative power of God's word, which "is living, active, and sharper than any two-edged sword" (Hebrews 4:12). Their messages convey God's will and help set into motion the process of making God's intentions real. The prophets do not speak mere words; their words are a creative force. The circumstances and content may vary, but every prophetic message holds the past, the present, and the future within itself. Each message rests on the foundation of God's history with God's people. Each speaks to the present moment. Each participates in and proclaims what's to come.

The prophets call their messages "the LORD's word," a "burden" (KJV), or an "oracle." Each term means essentially the same thing: It's a direct message from God to be lifted up to God's people. How the prophet originally received the message is not explained in detail. Sometimes they saw (for example, Micah 1:1; Zechariah 1:7-8) as well as heard with prophetic clarity. It was a spiritual, mental, and, sometimes, physical communication from God. It was also not just for the prophets' benefit. These extraordinary experiences must be passed on as the revealed word for God's people.

Because the prophet's voice was God's voice when the message was delivered, the nouns and pronouns sometimes shift quickly. The first chapter of Micah holds a good example. Micah begins by referring to "the LORD" in the third-person: "The LORD is coming out from his place" (verse 3). Micah then changes to the first person: "I [the LORD] will make Samaria a pile of rubble" (verse 6). Then, he shifts again, so that the "I" is now Micah: "I will cry out and howl" (verse 8). Though the nouns and pronouns may change unexpectedly, God is the true speaker and source of the message.

Receiving a word from God can be an overwhelming experience for the prophet. His heart, mind, spirit, voice—everything about him is caught up in being God's spokesman. It is similar to the way the apostle Paul described his new life in Christ: "I no longer live, but Christ lives in me. And the life that I now live in my body, I live by faith" (Galatians 2:20). The prophets did indeed live by faith. They offered their whole selves in service to God for as long as God needed them.

God's word that was revealed to the prophets has special impact and creative force beyond ordinary speech. Even so, the prophets' vocabulary and the way they shaped their messages were familiar to their listeners. There is no "speaking in tongues" as our saying goes, as if it was a foreign language needing translation. For example,

- The Minor Prophets offer prayers and praise to God like people are used to hearing in worship. Habakkuk sings, "LORD, I have heard your reputation, / I have seen your work.... The LORD God is my strength" (3:2a, 19a).

• They lament their own fates and that of their people. Habakkuk asks, "LORD, how long will I call for help and you not listen?" (1:2). "I [the LORD] will stretch out my hand against Judah / and against all the inhabitants of Jerusalem," declares Zephaniah (1:4).

• They remind people of God's power over creation. Haggai proclaims, "I [the LORD] have called for drought on the earth" (1:11).

• They recount God's goodness to God's chosen people in the past: "You will know that I [the LORD] have sent this command to you / so that my covenant with Levi can continue.... My covenant with him involved life and peace" (Malachi 2:4-5).

• They remind their listeners that God's expectations of them are no big surprise: "He has told you, human one, what is good and / what the LORD requires from you" (Micah 6:8).

Two other types of prophetic messages may not be quite as familiar. Vision reports tell of extraordinary "seeing" by the prophet (for example, Zechariah 1:7–6:15). In these messages, the prophet may see heavenly beings as well as human beings and familiar objects. The meaning of each visionary detail may not be clear to the prophet or his listeners, but the larger point is still made: God is at work and in charge, in both the heavenly realm and in human history.

Sign acts are another out-of-the-ordinary form of prophetic communication. These are demonstrations or the symbolic acting out of a truth that God wants people to know. For example, Micah stripped off his clothes and walked around howling with grief over the destruction coming to his people (1:8). Habakkuk was told to write his vision on a tablet so that it was plain even to someone hurrying by (2:2).

Many of the Minor Prophets' messages are announcements of judgment. Some are structured like lawsuits, with which people are familiar. All emphasize the logic and justice of God's case against his people. Micah 3:9-12 is a classic example:

- call to pay attention: "Hear this" (verse 9)
- who is being judged: "leaders of the house of Jacob" (verse 9)
- description of sins: "who reject justice" (verse 9)
- connection between sin and punishment: "Therefore, because of you" (verse 12)
- declaration of punishment: "Jerusalem will become piles of rubble" (verse 12)

Prophetic announcements of hope balance the ones of judgment and give people a haven against total despair. For example, Nahum 1:12-13 proclaims Assyria's doom and Zion's rescue:

- call to attention: "The LORD proclaims" (verse 12)
- who is addressed: "Zion" (verse 12)
- reason for hope: "They [the Assyrians] have been cut off" (verse 12)
- promise of relief: "I [the Lord] won't afflict you further" (verse 12)

The prophets loved God and loved their people, but they did not live above frustration or even anger with those who had hard heads and hard hearts. Some of their messages have a satirical tone and ask of their listeners, "Are you really *that* out of touch with reality?" Habakkuk asks bluntly, "Of what value is an idol?" (2:18). He then drives home the point that idol worship is nonsensical, saying, "The potter trusts the pottery, / though it is incapable of speaking. / Doom to the one saying to the tree, 'Wake up!' / or 'Get up' to the silent stone" (Habakkuk 2:18-19). All of the prophets show their feelings and do not shy away from the fallen state of their community.

Being called and set apart in God's service does not protect us from the reality of sin. On the contrary, it can force us to confront the sad state of humankind in ways we never before imagined. While the prophets had great spiritual gifts and exceptional relationships with God, they still lived in the down-and-dirty world of war, sin, grief, and foolishness.

Called to Care

The Minor Prophets loved and cared about God, who was the Lord and Master of their lives. They also cared about their brothers and sisters in the community of faith. They cared about the survival of God's chosen people. That being said, it is not easy to tell people you love that they are wrong and that something terrible is coming. No wonder the prophets' messages are called "a burden."

As God's messengers, the prophets were also intercessors, seeking reconciliation between God and God's people. They wanted the people to be reconciled to their destiny. They explained that what was happening to them all went back to their lack of faithfulness to God. The Minor Prophets reconciled the present with the past, always coming back to the consequences of breaking the covenant and not listening to God. They knew God's punishment to be reasonable and just. The people could and must accept that before things could get better. The Minor Prophets also sought to reconcile what people were seeing in the present to what was coming, whether it was punishment or redemption. They said, in effect, "Expand your vision. Get out of your limited way of living. See and hear what the living God has for you. Come back to the true God and to your true selves as God's people."

Called to Teach

Whenever God speaks, we can know God better. The Minor Prophets told the Israelites and tell us what God is up to and what it means for us. The Minor Prophets remind their listeners and readers about what God says and does in the past in order to make the present clear. We all need to know God better. We all need to listen for God's voice and look at ourselves in the light of God's word.

The Minor Prophets say that God is always interested in our good. God is all about life, peace, wholeness, righteousness, and justice. How we treat God and one another matters. God has high standards, and we suffer when we let those standards lapse. The Minor Prophets do not hide our ugliness and sin. They mince no words when confronting us with that part of our nature.

However, the Minor Prophets never leave us without hope. They say over and over again that God moves through history and through our lives with the ultimate goal of salvation and redemption for God's people.

Live the Story

Abraham Lincoln was a renowned storyteller. He once recounted the tale of a traveler on the frontier who found himself in rough terrain one night. A terrific thunderstorm broke out. His horse refused to go on, and so the man had to proceed on foot in the dark and lead the animal as best he could. The peals of thunder were frightful, and only the lightning afforded him clues to find his way. One bolt, which seemed to shatter the earth beneath him, brought the man to his knees. He wasn't a praying man, but he issued a short and clear petition: "Oh Lord! If it's all the same to you, give us a little more light and a little less noise!"[1]

We might often join the Minor Prophets to utter a similar prayer. While the Minor Prophets are certainly about shedding light on the way for God's people, they also lived in mighty "noisy" times. We may also live in such times, whether personally or as a community of faith. The Minor Prophets show us that it is both possible and absolutely necessary for us to live by the light God sends us, even in stormy times when we are scared and uncertain.

They show us that fidelity to God's way and God's call is essential. They kept the faith even when the call was to a difficult task, even when they were angry or afraid. Can we say "OK" to God when the call is ours to speak and act for God?

Perhaps even harder, can we be good listeners? Can we willingly be on the receiving end of a prophetic word? Our own hard call might be to hear, to truly hear, instead of to speak. The Minor Prophets asked their listeners to be open to hearing an old truth in a new light. They ask the same thing of us because our spiritual "GPS units" need regular updating.

The Minor Prophets rely on our God-given ability to choose. In the midst of our sometimes stormy, sinful lives, do we choose God's light and God's way?

---

1. From *Lincoln's Melancholy: How Depression Challenged a President and Fueled His Greatness*, by Joshua Wolf Shenk (Houghton Mifflin Company, 2005); page 118.

2.

Micah: A Regular Guy "Who Is Like the Lord"

Micah

Claim Your Story

Staunton Harold Church stands amidst beautiful parkland in Leicestershire, England. Its impressive Gothic-style stonework, stained-glass windows, and richly decorated interior attest to its builder's commitment to his faith and his church. Seeing it today, in such a peaceful setting, you might not guess that it was built in very tumultuous times that were unfriendly to the established church.

Sir Robert Shirley founded Staunton Harold Church in 1653, between England's civil war and the restoration of the monarchy. Also known as the Chapel of the Holy Trinity, Staunton Harold is literally Shirley's home church in that it stands next to his house. He committed his time, money, and, as it turned out, his life to this outward and visible sign of his faith in God.

When Oliver Cromwell, the Commonwealth leader, heard of Shirley's construction project, he decided that Shirley could very well make a contribution toward a naval vessel if he could afford so fine a church. When Shirley refused this demand, he was imprisoned and died there without ever seeing his church completed.[1]

An inscription above its west door honors his memory and faith:

In the year 1653 when all things Sacred were throughout ye nation, Either demolisht or profaned, Sir Robert Shirley, Baronet, Founded this church; Whose singular praise it is, to have done the best things in ye worst times, and hoped them in the most callamitous. The righteous shall be had in everlasting remembrance.[2]

Like Robert Shirley, Micah also deserves our "singular praise." He dedicated his life to speak for God, exposing himself to scorn and rejection, even death, during his own calamitous times. He was God's messenger. It was who he had to be. Rather than taking the easy way out, he was faithful to his calling.

The end of Shirley's inscription is taken from Psalm 112:6: "The righteous shall be in everlasting remembrance" (KJV). It affirms the truth that our faithfulness in this life does matter. God sees and remembers.

Do we say "yes" to God even in the worst of times? Do we live as if we know our calling and to whom we owe our ultimate allegiance? Micah's life and ministry bring us face to face with questions about who we are and what we stand for.

Enter the Bible Story

Micah's Times

We see Micah now as an extraordinary person who is acclaimed as one of the great prophets of his time. However, before his prophetic ministry began, Micah (whose name in Hebrew means "Who is like the Lord?") was someone we might call "a regular guy." He was not part of the political or prophetic establishment. Neither his lineage nor his credentials is cited in Scripture. We just know his name and where he was from. Micah could have been a farmer or tradesman, perhaps known in his community for his faith and good works. He lived about twenty-five miles southwest of Jerusalem in Moresheth, which sat near both east-west and north-south trade routes in Judah. This location gave Micah the opportunity to hear news of the wider world from travelers, tradesmen, and soldiers.

There is no doubt that the times brought him disturbing news. To the north, the nation of Israel was in turmoil, with rampant corruption, injustice, and tolerance of pagan worship. Judah was also struggling, and both nations had to deal with Assyria, which was determined to conquer Israel and bring Judah to heel.

As we know, God calls prophets for hard times, and Micah's task was full of risk and heartache. Micah knew Israel's history, which included disrespect for and abuse of her prophets. Micah also knew the law. When he left his everyday life to speak for God, he must have realized that it may cost him his life. Nevertheless, he was ready to "compete in the good fight of faith" (1 Timothy 6:12).

About the Scriptures

Dangers of Speaking the Truth

Old Testament law specifies that false prophecy is punishable by death (Deuteronomy 18:20). Though Micah spoke the truth from the Lord, enemies of the truth sought to silence him. Corrupt leaders, priests, and prophets still recognized the power of what Micah said, and they didn't want things to change. They wanted to maintain their hold on power and profit. If they could convince the king and others that Micah was a false prophet, they could get rid of him (Micah 2:6-7).

Generations later, Jeremiah also faced the possibility of death at the hands of those who opposed his message. His defenders used Micah as an example of a prophet who faced potentially lethal consequences for his faithful service to God (Jeremiah 26:12-19). In both their cases, God's truth won out, and the prophets continued their ministries.

Being a prophet is passionate, tough work. Micah loved the Lord with all his heart, being, and strength (Deuteronomy 6:5) in order to speak and persevere. When the Lord's word came to Micah, he saw a tragic future for his people. Their unfaithfulness was bringing destruction on themselves and their children. Thanks be to God, Micah also saw hope beyond the tragedy. He knew that God's love had the last word.

Micah's Messages

The Book of Micah maintains the conversational, vocal flavor of Micah's original messages. Just as we, in conversations and sermons, head one way, go off after another thought, and then come back, so does Micah. Proclamations of hope break out in the midst of his messages of judgment. At times he shifts from speaking with God's voice in the first person to speaking about God in the third person to talking about himself, but he is always giving us "the LORD's word" (Micah 1:1).

Micah had a great way with words. He used wordplays, puns, and vivid metaphors to get people's attention and help them remember what he said. These are not always evident in English, so reading more than one translation of the text can help bring out Micah's mastery of the language. For example, James Moffatt's translation of the first chapter showcases Micah's verbal skills:

- In declaring judgment on Samaria, God said that all her pagan idols and shrines would be destroyed by the Assyrians. What was "once the prize of faithless living, now the prey of faithless foes" (Micah 1:7).[3]
- Micah then named some of the towns that would be caught up in the destruction and warned their inhabitants of what lay in store: "Weep tears at Teartown (Bochim), grovel in the dust at Dustown (Beth-ophrah) / Fare forth stripped O Fairtown (Saphir)! Stirtown (Zaanan) dare not stir, / Beth-esel . . . and Maroth hopes in vain; for doom descends from the Eternal to the very gates of Jerusalem . . . and Israel's kings are ever balked at Balkton (Achzib)" (Micah 1:10-14).[4]

Micah sometimes used what is called the "prophetic perfect tense of vision."[5] This means he spoke of the future as if it had already happened. In Micah 1:16, he instructs the people of Judah to mourn for their children who will be carried into exile in Babylon over one hundred years later. He says, "They have gone from you," because it is as good as done.

Micah proclaimed God's judgment against the people of Israel because of their sins, and he described the coming destruction. Beyond the punishment, Micah saw a time of redemption for Israel and the world. Micah also shared his deep, personal faith. Even though punishment was at hand and redemption far off, he said, in effect, "Yes, things are bad, but the Lord is my strength and I will trust him no matter what."

Micah's Messages of Judgment

Micah wasted no time in letting us know the scope and consequences of human sin. In the first chapter, after a one-verse introduction of the prophet, the Lord of creation takes center stage and calls all the earth to hear the case against God's people. God is witness, prosecutor, and judge. Nothing is hidden from God, and nothing is beyond God's control. Micah left no doubt about what was happening and what was at stake. People in the nation of Israel and in Judah were worshipping idols instead of the one true God. Because of this, Samaria and Jerusalem would be demolished and become fit only for farmland (Micah 1:6; 3:12). Even the Temple would not be spared. Faithfulness and righteousness are more precious to God than the Holy City, Zion, or any shrine that human hands can build.

Next up on Micah's "hit list" are theft, corruption, false prophecy, violence, and giving only lip service to God and the covenant. He singled out leaders and judges, priests, and prophets who were mindful only of their personal power and material gain. They are "those who devise wickedness" (Micah 2:1).

Leaders manipulated the law to steal property and drive women and children from their homes (Micah 2:2, 9). Officials and judges demanded bribes so that the rich and powerful got their way at others' expense (Micah 3:11; 7:3). Even priests and prophets used their positions of authority to enrich themselves (Micah 2:11; 3:5, 11). They used God's good name as a cover for their crimes and falsehoods. Merchants used false weights to cheat their customers while people routinely abused one another and lied (Micah 6:11-12). They didn't want to hear the truth and sought to silence God's messenger (Micah 2:6).

Even close relationships between family members and friends were filled with betrayal: "The enemies of a man are those of his own household" (Micah 7:2-6). Micah characterized the leaders in Israel as cannibals who devoured those they were supposed to guide and protect (Micah 3:1-3). "Isn't it your job to know justice?" he asked. Instead, they perverted righteousness and justice into something horrifying.

"Therefore," said the Lord, another kind of terror and destruction was coming. Micah 3:9-12 summarizes God's case against God's people and proves the justice of what was to come. Their sins and crimes were bringing destruction of everyone, the righteous and unrighteous alike.

We may want to protest how God handles such situations. Why should the righteous also suffer? How is that just? But, as people are fond of saying these days, it is what it is. Because God created us to be in relationship with God and with one another, our connections with one another sometimes bring pain through no fault of our own.

Micah's Messages of Hope

Micah does not leave his people, or us, bereft of hope. Micah 4:1-4 gives a beautiful and eloquent description of God's purposes for all peoples. He tells of "days to come" when God will bring not destruction but peace and plenty. Corrupt judges will be gone. God and God's house will draw friend and foe alike, so that everyone will seek and find the true word of instruction and justice.

The old gospel hymn "Down by the Riverside" celebrates such a time. Everyone will say, "Goin't' lay down my sword and shield," and "Ain't goin't' study war no more."[6] No longer will anyone terrify us. From a tragedy of our own making, God will redeem us and will bring us home (Micah 4:6-8). Micah reassures us that we will "walk in the name of the LORD our God forever and always" (Micah 4:5).

Micah has even more good news, however. He gives us a glimpse of the Messiah (Micah 5:2-5a), who, like Micah, will come from a small, out-of-the-way town. He will be a ruler for Israel on God's behalf to bring security and peace to God's people. Matthew 2:6 and John 7:42 refer to this prophecy in which Micah foretells the coming of Jesus. Micah sees that distant day when our ultimate King comes to "shepherd his flock in the strength of the LORD" and will "become great throughout the earth" (Micah 5:4).

All is not lost for God's people. The fruit of Micah's labor was penitence and confession in Zion (Micah 7:8-9). The people admitted the justice of God's case against them, and they affirmed their faith that God would bring them out into the light because of God's righteousness.

Micah interceded with God on behalf of his people (Micah 7:14). When God replied that "wonderful things" were in Israel's future, Micah responded with his own affirmation of faith and praise for God, who pardons sin, has compassion for God's people, and always "delights in faithful love" (Micah 7:15-20).

Micah's Faith

Micah may "cry out and howl" (Micah 1:8) and even shout, "I'm doomed!" (Micah 7:1) while he carried the burden of his prophecy. Even the most faithful of us are sometimes overwhelmed with frustration and fear. Nevertheless, Micah did not give up. He talked to God and patiently expected an answer (Micah 7:7). He was listening and looking in the right direction for wisdom and strength.

Admittedly, there are times when we do not look in the right direction, and there may be days when the best we can do is be a negative example for others. In a comic strip from a daily newspaper, a husband and wife are in conversation. He is filling out a crossword puzzle, has been chewing on his pen, and has ink all around his mouth. She says, "I told you not to chew on that ballpoint pen. That ink won't wash off, you know." He replies, "Oh, well, you know what they say . . . you live and you learn." She retorts, "This is at least the third time you've done this." "Okay," he concedes, "so some of us just *live*."[7]

So, according to Micah, how are we to both live and learn?

[The Lord] has told you, human one,
    what is good and
what the LORD requires from you:
    to do justice, embrace faithful love,
      and walk humbly with your God. (Micah 6:8)

Formalities are not the answer (Micah 6:6-7). God wants us, not in form only, but in reality and relationship.

We are to "do justice," not to lie, cheat, and steal, but to treat one another with respect. "Therefore," said Jesus, "you should treat people in the same way that you want people to treat you; this is the Law and the Prophets" (Matthew 7:12).

We are to "embrace faithful love," which includes goodness, mercy, and kindness. We joyfully welcome the opportunity to live out the Great Commandment: "Jesus replied, 'The most important [commandment] is *Israel, listen! Our God is the one Lord, and you must love the Lord your God with all your heart, with all your being, with all your mind, and with all your strength. The second is this, You will love your neighbor as yourself'*" (Mark 12:29-31).

We are to "walk humbly with [our] God." This beautiful image of walking with God brings to mind the garden of Eden. "During that day's cool evening breeze, [Adam and Eve] heard the sound of the LORD God walking in the garden" (Genesis 3:8). From the beginning, our Creator desires close, personal contact with us. Our walk, our life, is a journey in which God is always willing to remain beside us. As we walk with God, we are to be humble, obedient, and teachable. Adam and Eve, the people of Israel, and we suffer the consequences when we are arrogant and disobedient.

This walk of ours is not just moving and doing. It is based on an attitude of faith and trust, a total commitment of mind, body, and spirit. Micah tells us that we must remember and live out what we already know to be true. Micah makes it plain that "[God] has told you" over and over again.

For his part, God always remembers us and keeps faith with us. "If we confess our sins, he is faithful and just to forgive us our sins and cleanse us from everything we've done wrong" (1 John 1:9).

In the thick of battle, with troubles all around, Micah said with confidence, "I am filled with power, / with the spirit of the LORD" (Micah 3:8). He was filled with God's Spirit, with power to speak "not with words taught by human wisdom but with words taught by the Spirit" (1 Corinthians 2:12-13). Micah and the Spirit offer us that same power.

Live the Story

In setting up a voice mail greeting, we have great leeway in both style and content. Some of us just opt for a generic message provided by the phone company in someone else's voice. In our own voices we may be short and business-like, warm and friendly, or even take a moment to wish a caller "blessings on your day" as one minister does. A psychotherapist once had a greeting that probably made many of his callers hesitate before leaving their messages. He presented them with this opportunity and challenge: "Who are you? And what do you want? Many people spend their entire lives answering these questions. Please leave a message."

That sounds like a greeting Micah might have for us. He gives us the chance to reflect on who created us and who has sustained us in the past. He stands in the present day and confronts us with the futility of life apart from God. Without God we are perplexed, confused, and on the road destruction. It isn't that we don't know better. Micah looks us squarely in the eye and says, "God has *told* you what is good and what God requires from each of us." Paul also tells us bluntly, "Humans are without excuse" (Romans 1:20).

We are without excuse but not without hope. Micah assures us that God offers hope for a fresh start and a better day.

So, who are we? Are we really God's humble children? Like Robert Shirley, can we do the best things in the worst times and hope for God's best in the most calamitous? What do we want? More to the point, who do we want? Do we want God above all else?

1. From *http://www.nationaltrust.org.uk/wra-1356309414924/view-page/item504782/*.
2. From *http://www.nationaltrust.org.uk/wra-1356309414924/view-page/item504782/*.
3. From *A New Translation of the Bible Containing the Old and New Testaments*, by James Moffatt (Harper and Row Publishers, 1954); page 1009.
4. From *A New Translation of the Bible Containing the Old and New Testaments*; page 1009.
5. From *The New Interpreter's Bible One Volume Commentary* (Abingdon Press, 2010); page 515.
6. From "Down by the Riverside," in *The Cokesbury Worship Hymnal* (Abingdon Press, 1966); 259.
7. From *Pickles*, by Brian Crane (Washington Post Writers Group, July 18, 2003).

8.

Nahum, Habakkuk, and Zephaniah: The Perils of Power and Pride

Nahum, Habakkuk, and Zephaniah

Claim Your Story

The term *superpower* is often used to describe the United States' status among the nations of the world. For decades the U.S. has wielded military, political, economic, and cultural muscle to foster and protect its interests worldwide. Superpower status is both relative and changeable, however, and some now think that the United States' preeminent position is slipping. Other nations, such as China and India, are building their own strength and influence across the globe and are potential superpowers.

Military muscle and economic influence were constantly in play in the biblical world, too. During the time of Nahum, Habakkuk, and Zephaniah, Judah was a weaker player internationally, with Assyria's superpower status waning and Babylon coming on strong. Internally, the Judean political and religious elites often abused their positions to enrich themselves at others' expense.

In both the modern and biblical worlds, great power often breeds supersized pride. The prophets spent a lot of time talking about power, pride, and the trouble they can bring. The writer of Proverbs also knew the pitfalls of human pride: "Pride comes before disaster, / and arrogance before a fall" (Proverbs 16:18). They all would probably agree with C. S. Lewis, who declared, "Pride leads to every other vice: it is the complete anti-God state of mind."[1]

A March 2013 search of the online retailer Amazon.com revealed approximately 290,000 books with the word *power* in the title. *Control* appeared in over 200,000 titles. *Pride* came in a distant third with only about 12,000. Apparently these are topics of great interest to many of us!

The prophets were also interested in power, pride, and control. They want us to understand that God is the only true "superpower." God is in control and very much present in the world. How we act toward one another and toward God is crucial, and if things go wrong, God will act decisively to make things right once more. We can be "anti-God" only so long before the ugly consequences catch up with us.

Enter the Bible Story

Challenging Messages for Challenging Times

Nahum, Habakkuk, and Zephaniah were contemporaries of Jeremiah. Beginning in about 640 B.C. with Zephaniah until about 572 B.C. with the end of Jeremiah's ministry, God provided abundant prophetic leadership to help people get through these turbulent days. The nation of Israel had been absorbed into Assyria, and Judah was under strong Assyrian influence. Idol worship and dishonesty continued to flourish.

Zephaniah proclaimed that the "day of the LORD" (1:7) was coming as punishment for these sins. As Assyria's power waned, Nahum announced its violent end at the hands of the Babylonians. At the same time, Jeremiah saw trouble from Babylon on the horizon for the people of Judah. He knew that because of Judah's sins, Assyria's tyranny and corrupting influence were just being replaced by others. Habakkuk mocked those who worshipped idols, but much like Jeremiah, he was weary of trouble and wondered if God still cared about God's people. In the end, all the prophets put their trust in God and staked their lives on God's faithfulness to those who obey him. Underneath all their weariness and their questions rested a solid foundation of faith.

Lord, How Long?

The books of Nahum, Habakkuk, and Zephaniah are relatively short, with just three chapters each. These small books pack a punch, however. They are filled with graphic images of war and death, of violence on the battlefield and moral failures in everyday life. These prophets give us a vivid picture of God at his most wrathful. Some of it makes very unpleasant reading as we are confronted in verse after verse with God's overwhelming anger and determination to deal with sin. We may wonder if this is really our God. Does God condone the deaths of innocent children? How do the prophets maintain their own faith and trust in God when they announce such things on God's behalf? One way that Habakkuk deals with this is by bluntly asking God, "LORD, how long will I call for help and you not listen?" and "Why would you...keep silent when the wicked swallows one who is more righteous?" (Habakkuk 1:2, 13). The prophets show us that we have the freedom to question God. They also show us that we have the responsibility to know God better.

It may not be easy to grasp the whole picture of God that these prophets present. It is necessary, however, not to shy away from the hard parts. Scripture tells us that to know God truly, we must accept that "the beginning of wisdom is the fear of the LORD; / the knowledge of the holy one is understanding" (Proverbs 9:10). We do not cower before God, but we do stand in awe of God's holiness and majesty. The Bible is very clear that God is the Creator who holds the ultimate power of death and life. Moses also makes it plain that if you turn away from God, "you will definitely die" (Deuteronomy 30:18).

The latter prophets' messages echo Moses' instructions. God is to be respected and obeyed. The prophets are also adamant that God's high standards are not too difficult for us (for example, Micah 6:8; also Joshua 24:14-15). God never asks us to do what is impossible. Over and over again, the prophets clearly tell us that it is our choice to walk in God's ways and keep our hearts true to God. We may never understand why the innocent suffer or be able to accept it without question. We can, however, take seriously our own walk with God. We can humbly accept God's sovereignty over our lives, keep our pride in check, and use our power at God's direction.

Across the Testaments

A Love That Sees Us Through Any Trial

Suffering and the questions it brings are unavoidable. The apostle Paul, who knew the Law and the Prophets inside out, did not try to explain away suffering (Romans 8:35-38). Rather, he approached it as part of life. He assured us, however, that we would "win a sweeping victory" (verse 37) over trouble through the love of Jesus. God's love for us in Christ Jesus is stronger than anything life can throw at us, and not even death can break God's hold on us ("nothing can separate us from God's love in Christ Jesus our Lord," verse 38).

In the midst of his own suffering, Paul looked beyond it to a greater reality: "I believe that the present suffering is nothing compared to the coming glory that is going to be revealed to us" (Romans 8:18).

First Peter 4:12-13 admonishes, "Dear friends, don't be surprised about the fiery trials that have come among you to test you. These are not strange happenings. Indeed, rejoice as you share Christ's suffering."

As difficult as it is to accept, hard times can also be for our own good, because God loves us enough to test and discipline us. Revelation 3:19 says, "I [Jesus] correct and discipline those whom I love. So be earnest and change your hearts and lives." Sometimes it takes discipline, a time of trial, or outright suffering to bring us closer to God.

Nahum, Habakkuk, and Zephaniah, like their fellow prophets, also have messages of hope for God's people. They point to God's plans for the restoration of righteousness and justice among all nations. They never leave us without assurances of God's mercy, love, and willingness to hear our cries. Even though prophets confront us with things we would rather not face, they also tell us that all is not lost. God's justifiable wrath may be certain, but grace and redemption always follow.

After all our confusion, anguish, and searching for answers, we come back to what Moses tells us. Love the Lord your God, obey God's voice, and cling to God (Deuteronomy 30:20). Zephaniah tells us to "seek the LORD, all you humble of the land who practice his justice; / seek righteousness; / seek humility" (Zephaniah 2:3). We can also follow Peter's lead. As a disciple, he was confronted with the choice to stick with Jesus or walk away. He made his choice and his confession: "Lord, to whom shall we go? You have the words (the message) of eternal life" (John 6:68, AMP). We can do the same.

Nahum

Nahum's focus was on Nineveh, the capital of Assyria. The nations of Israel and Judah as well as others had suffered under Assyrian military might and tyrannical influence. Now the tables were beginning to turn because in God's eyes, Assyria had been excessively cruel (Nahum 3:19). It had gone too far in preying on other nations, and now that nation itself would be prey (2:11–3:1).

In the first chapter, the prophet uses very strong adjectives to describe God as the Lord of creation and enemy of sinners. God is jealous, vengeful, powerful, indignant, furious, wrathful, and destructive. God annihilates and afflicts both the chosen people and others. As a rushing flood, God will "pursue his enemies into darkness" (1:8). Neither the mountains nor any human being can match God's power.

In vivid, cinematic images, Nahum proclaims what is coming for Nineveh (3:1-3, 10). He describes human military might at its most powerful and destructive. The Assyrians had destroyed other nations. They also had enjoyed great economic prosperity, with traders more numerous "than the heavens have stars" (3:16). Now, however, their dominance was ending.

Neither their military might nor their economic power was a match for "the LORD of heavenly forces" (2:13; 3:5). Relentlessly Nahum and the other prophets force us to look beyond the world of flesh, blood, chariots, and money. That world is strong, for sure, but not as strong as the world of the Spirit. We may believe we are smart, strong, and successful, and that we can keep things going our way. If we believe and live that way, the prophets are ready to enlarge our perspectives and show us we are wrong.

Though Nahum's message is like a whirlwind of vengeance, he also says that God is patient, good, and mindful of those who keep the faith (1:3, 7). God is a haven for those in distress and our only true source of hope and security. Through this fierce prophet, God announces a future time of peace, restoration, and renewal of true worship (1:15).

Habakkuk

The Book of Habakkuk opens with a conversation between God and a very frustrated, impatient prophet. Habakkuk was faithfully fulfilling his duty to see and proclaim God's word. For all his efforts, he felt alone, scared, tired, and puzzled. He was sick of what God was showing him and did not think that God was doing enough to fix the situation. Fellow prophet Jeremiah also was not shy about telling God in no uncertain terms what his prophetic duty was costing him. He said, "The LORD's word has brought me nothing but insult and injury, constantly" (Jeremiah 20:8).

Habakkuk's opening question is one many of us ask: "LORD, how long will I call for help and you not listen?" (Habakkuk 1:2). Well, God was listening, and God told Habakkuk just to be quiet and pay attention (1:5). But despite God's instructions, Habakkuk wouldn't be quiet. He affirmed that the Chaldeans were coming "for judgment" against Judah, and he knew that it would be terrible (1:12-17). He told God all this as if God did not truly appreciate the seriousness of the situation! The prophet then freely admitted he was complaining, and he finally got quiet, ready to hear God's response (2:1).

God made things plain to Habakkuk, who was to present God's message so that even someone in a hurry couldn't miss it (2:2). The message, as always, was on God's terms and in God's time. God's reasons for sending punishment on Judah were all too familiar: idol worship, greed, plunder, injustice, and arrogance. The generations since Micah's prophecy continued in their sinful ways (Micah 6:1–7:7). God mocked those who ignored him in favor of their own creations. "Doom to the one saying to the tree, 'Wake up!' / or 'Get up' to the silent stone. / Does it teach?" (Habakkuk 2:19). The idol does not teach us anything except our own foolishness. It is the living, Creator God who teaches us the truth. If we sin against God, we sin against our own lives (2:10-11). Our lives are bound up with God, and apart from God we can do nothing (John 15:5).

There is hope, however. God does have pity on us in spite of our sin and futile ways of living. One day, in God's time, "the land will be full of the knowledge of the LORD's glory" (Habakkuk 2:14). God comes to his temple among his people, and there are no more questions or complaints, just a fulfilled, respectful silence for the Lord. In conclusion, Habakkuk admitted his fear and trembling as he waited for God's deliverance (3:16). As he waited, even facing famine and starvation, he would trust God and rejoice (3:17-19).

Zephaniah

Zephaniah had an impressive family tree. He was a descendent of King Hezekiah of Judah (715–687 B.C.), and his family may have been among the political and religious elite in Jerusalem. He may have had every right to be proud of his heritage and position in society, but Zephaniah was first and foremost God's servant.

He announced God's judgment on all humanity, specifically on Judah and Jerusalem for idol worship and turning away from God (Zephaniah 1:4-6). Too many people did not "seek the LORD" and thought that God was irrelevant. They said, "The LORD won't do good or evil" (1:12). Zephaniah cried "doom" over Jerusalem (3:1), which was supposed to be God's holy city, but instead was obstinate in its sins, defiled by idol worship, prideful, full of violence, and disobedient even in the face of God's discipline (3:1-8).

Zephaniah specifically condemned princes, judges, prophets, and priests who served at God's discretion but who betrayed the people's trust. Priests even did "violence" to God's Word ("the Instruction," 3:4) by giving perverse rulings on religious matters that benefited only themselves. God's innate righteousness and justice are offended by such blatant sin and disrespect. Those who got up early to practice corruption were in for a very rude awakening indeed (3:7-8). Other nations did not escape God's justice either (2:4-15). God controls the natural world as well as human history, so no one is beyond God's reach, even if he or she does not believe in God.

Zephaniah announced "the day of the LORD," which is a day of divine judgment against Judah and other nations (Zephaniah 1:7, 10, 14; 2:2; 3:8; also Nahum 1:7; Habakkuk 3:16). This is not the final judgment at the end of time (for example, Matthew 24:31-51), but is an imminent day of chastisement for sin. In horrific images, Zephaniah described the toll exacted for human sin (Zephaniah 1:14-17). He echoed the prophet Amos that this day of reckoning brings darkness and death (Amos 5:18-20). All our money, fine cities, military hardware, and deluded pride cannot help us in the end. Nothing can stand up to God's holy might. Isaiah 2:12 also announces, "The LORD of heavenly forces has planned a day; / against all that is prideful and haughty."

On the other side of judgment, there will be another "day of the LORD" that brings redemption and renewal (Zephaniah 3:9-20). There will be survivors among God's people who will have the chance to make a new start. But first, the wages of sin must be paid.

Live the Story

A Jewish proverb declares, "God waits long, but He pays with interest."[2] Nahum, Habakkuk, and Zephaniah tell us that one way or the other, the "day of the LORD" is payday. There are two paydays, one for judgment and one for redemption, but they emphasize Judgment Day and its consequences. Jeremiah also knew a terrible day of reckoning was at hand. Through him, God asked his people, "Isn't my word like fire and like a hammer that shatters rock?" (Jeremiah 23:29). All the prophets declare God's intention to bring the hammer down on disobedience, pride, and violence.

Patience is hard for most of us, especially since instant gratification is now seen as almost a universal right. Suffering tests our patience and our faith that God will help us. The payday of redemption may appear far away or only for someone else. Can we remain faithful while we wait? Can we stop asking God "why" and look for what God has to teach us? Faithful patience allows us to see God at work while we wait.

On the other hand, we are not always the innocent ones. As the comic strip *Pogo* famously puts it, "We have met the enemy, and he is us."[3] The cross of Christ offers us forgiveness when we are "the enemy," but we still have to account for ourselves to God. Can we remember that God's discipline and tests are for our ultimate good?

The prophets confront us over and over again with questions about power and how we use it. Are our limited and temporary powers put at God's disposal and used according to God's will? The prophets also hold us accountable for our prideful hearts. Do we humbly recognize God as the highest authority in our lives?

Nahum, Habakkuk, and Zephaniah enlarge our perspectives and question our priorities. They prompt us to take the larger view—God's view—of life and eternity. They ask us to match their devotion to God. To what or to whom are we most devoted? Idol worship can be insidious and includes much more than strange rituals or expecting guidance from a rock. Is God really our first and greatest love?

Taking the prophets' messages seriously means taking a hard look at ourselves. They ask us to consider what kind of interest we are expecting on God's payday.

1. From *Mere Christianity*, by C.S. Lewis (The Macmillan Company, 1960); page 109.
2. From *Leo Rosten's Treasury of Jewish Quotations*, by Leo Rosten (Bantam Books, 1980); page 220.
3. From *Pogo: We Have Met the Enemy and He Is Us*, by Walt Kelly (Simon & Schuster, 1972).

4.

Nahum, Habakkuk, and Zephaniah: Hope for Castoffs

Nahum, Habakkuk, and Zephaniah

Claim Your Story

The Reverend Howard Finster (c. 1915–2001) called himself a "man of visions." He shared these visions with the world through his incredible sacred art. A lay pastor and bicycle repairman, Finster felt God's call to produce his faith-inspired artwork after seeing a face in a dab of paint on his finger. From 1976 until his death at age 84, Finster created more than 47,000 works, including paintings, sculpture, architecture, and mosaics. His preaching found new expression as he proclaimed the gospel in bold images and words that won him international acclaim.

Finster's Northwest Georgia home is called Paradise Garden. Finster filled its buildings and grounds to overflowing with tangible representations of his "visions of other worlds." He often used cast-off objects in his installations, finding beauty where others saw only trash to be discarded. He recognized the harsh realities of this life even as he used its castoffs to reveal God's greater, transcendent reality.[1]

In one of his paintings, Finster shows an angel pointing the way to heaven, to a part of God's creation that we can't see with mortal eyes. Next to the angel he writes, "Reach up and touch God with prayer. He loves you," and "Heaven is worth it all."

Nahum, Habakkuk, and Zephaniah also know that reality encompasses much more than our physical world. The prophets point us to a higher, better life that can only come from trust in God and putting God first. Though they make no excuses for sin and do not gloss over its consequences, they tell us that this is still God's world and that God's purposes—for us and for all of creation—are beautiful.

The prophets help us answer some tough questions. How do we stay faithful when we feel like castoffs? How do we catch a glimpse of God's heavenly reality? What do we really expect from God and hope for in the end?

Enter the Bible Story

So often it is easier for us to focus on what's wrong in our lives rather than on what's right. We are quicker to count our troubles than to count our blessings. Listening to the prophets can seem like more trouble than blessing and can be like having a bucket of cold water thrown in our faces. Their "wake-up calls" to us are tough and challenging. But that's not the whole story. The Minor Prophets are just as real about hope as they are about judgment.

Nahum

Nahum had a lot to say about pain, hatred, and bitterness. He does not spend much time telling us how to find beauty in the world unless it's in the destruction of our enemies. For a hundred years, Assyria had been a brutal master and corrupting religious influence in the lives of God's people. Micah describes how the Assyrian storm came to Israel and then to Judah because of faithless disregard for God's laws (Micah 1). The state of Israel disappeared into Assyria, and Judah suffered at their hands. Now, Nahum forcefully declared, payback time was at hand, and Judah's oppressors were about to get a taste of their own medicine. In God's eyes, they had gone too far in preying on other nations. God was witness, judge, and executioner against Assyrian violence and pride. As God's messenger, Nahum was unrelenting and unsparing in his descriptions of the coming terror. This may seem excessive to us, but truth be told, we might also feel great satisfaction when a hated foe is vanquished.

If there is any sweetness, any hope in Nahum and his message, we find it in these short verses:

- "The LORD is very patient but great in power; / the Lord punishes" (1:3).
- "The LORD is good, / a haven in a day of distress. / He acknowledges those who take refuge in him" (1:7).
- "I [the Lord] have afflicted you; / I won't afflict you further, Zion. / Now I will break off his yoke from you and tear off your chains" (1:12-13).
- "Look, on the mountains: the feet of a messenger who announces peace! / Celebrate your festivals, Judah! Fulfill your solemn promises! / The worthless one will never again invade you; / he has been completely cut off" (1:15).
- "The LORD will restore the pride of Jacob, / indeed, the pride of Israel, / because ravagers have destroyed them and spoiled their branches" (2:2).

God had sent affliction from the Assyrians, but their time was running out. Already the message of peace was there if people would have just stopped and listened. In the Lord's Prayer, we confess that "the kingdom, and the power, and the glory" belong to God (Matthew 6:13, KJV). In his own way, Nahum affirmed the same thing. He tells us that God holds the power to punish and to bless. Great power is God's alone and also great love, because God provides a haven for the faithful in days of trouble.

The people of Judah were not redeemed by their own strength or merit. It was by God's power and goodness that they rose from destruction. Pride was restored, but not the false, deadly pride that leads to ruin and alienation from God. This new pride was a gift from God. The Hebrew word for "pride" is very similar to the word for "vine." As a restored "vine," God's people can be fruitful. They can fulfill their promises to worship God with purity and joy.

Nahum was not all about vengeance and death. He saw a day when his people acknowledged God as their refuge and strength. The prophet expected them to worship God as their only Lord and fulfill their covenant promises. He looked forward to a day when they would be free and fruitful once again.

Habakkuk

Habakkuk made his personal walk with God part of his prophetic message. He questioned and argued with God, admitting his fears and frustrations as well as admitting he sometimes did not understand God's ways. This honesty makes his affirmations of hope and his ultimate expressions of confidence in God all the more genuine. His trust in God was not theoretical or based on a charmed life. Habakkuk's trust came out of a crucible of anger, doubt, and fear.

He also sounded tired. For generations, the prophets warned God's people about betraying God's trust. The Assyrians had wreaked havoc in their lives, the Babylonians were poised to continue the trend, and Judah did not seem to be listening to her prophets.

Even so, Habakkuk pleaded his case and then waited for God. In the midst of doom and discouragement, he heard this reassurance: "The land will be full of the knowledge of the LORD's glory, / just as water covers the sea" (2:14). And, "the LORD is in his holy temple. / Let all the earth be silent before him" (2:20).

Habakkuk was not silent for long, but this time, instead of complaints, he offered a prayer (3:1-19). He began with an affirmation of faith and a petition: "O LORD! I have learned of Your renown; / I am awed, O LORD, by Your deeds. Renew them in these years, / Oh, make them known in these years! / Though angry, may You remember compassion" (3:2).[2] Habakkuk then praised God's majesty and power, and he recounted God's mighty deeds (verses 3-15).

At the end, the prophet again declared his faith in God, no matter what might come (verses 16-19). Here was an honest man who loved and honored God but also admitted his profound fear and trembling. Despite the fear, he was also confident that God's "day of distress" would deliver his people from their enemies. Out of this confidence comes one of the most lyrical and beautiful affirmations of faith in the entire Bible: "Though the fig tree doesn't bloom, / and there's no produce on the vine; / though the olive crop withers, / and the fields don't provide food; / though the sheep is cut off from the pen, / and there is no cattle in the stalls; / I will rejoice in the LORD. / I will rejoice in the God of my deliverance. / The LORD God is my strength" (verses 17-19). War and starvation could not destroy his faith or cut him off from his true source of joy and strength. Habakkuk may have been walking through the darkest valley, but he knew that God would lead him and his people to the heights of redemption. His faith was a beacon of hope for others in dark times.

Habakkuk shows us how to come out of hiding, so to speak, and be honest with God about our fear and anger. Once we do that, Habakkuk tells us to be still, watch, and listen for God's reply. God does listen and answer. Habakkuk assures us that we are not alone.

Zephaniah

Hope is not hard to find in Zephaniah, though it's a lot quieter than punishment. The "great day" of the Lord's judgment against the world and Judah is loud and dramatic, full of fury and devouring fire. Even on the day of the Lord's anger, it is the quiet, humble ones who may escape the destruction (2:3). Those who seek God and practice justice, righteousness, and humility find a refuge in time of trouble.

God's day of hope and restoration is more subdued. There are shouts of joy among God's people, but no violent victory chants over fallen enemies. There are no human warriors to boast loudly about their triumph. God alone brings this victory and crowns it with singing and calming love (3:14-17).

God will tend to the survivors from Judah as a shepherd tends to his flock (2:7; also Jeremiah 23:3-4). When justice is served and the exile is over, a forgiven remnant will come home (Zephaniah 3:9-20). This remnant will be different from the stubborn, prideful, and unfaithful leaders that the prophet condemns. They will instead be a small, humble, powerless group who will probably look pitiful in the eyes of the world. They may be looked down on as dispossessed outcasts, but it's God's opinion that matters, and God has great plans for them.

The Reverend Howard Finster loved castoffs, which are the outcasts of our material culture. These "found objects," what we used to call trash, were at the heart of his artwork. He once addressed a poem to those who provided him this trove of material and inspiration:

I took the pieces you threw away
And put them together night and day
Washed by rain and dried by sun
A million pieces all in one.[3]

Finster's castoffs still inspire and delight us, but God's outcasts have even greater potential and beauty. From a humble and powerless people, God builds a community of faith to honor and worship God in spirit and in truth. There is hope in that for us, too. We may not be literal outcasts, but our own failures surely can bring us grief. When that happens, God offers to bring us back into the fold and to renew our hearts and minds for his own good purposes.

Across the Testaments

We Bring the Faith, God Brings the Power

The story of Jesus feeding five thousand people (Mark 6:30-44; John 6:1-13) also demonstrates what God can do with something that seems insufficient or is only fit to be discarded. Jesus had five loaves of bread and two fish with which to feed the crowd who had followed him to this isolated place. Jesus gave them living bread, which is the word of God, and now they needed literal bread at the end of the day. Jesus was given a small, seemingly inadequate amount of food. He looked to heaven, blessed the food, and broke it into pieces. Then there was plenty for everyone.

The disciples' first reaction to the situation was, "It's impossible to feed all these people!" Jesus' response was, "Just check to see what resources you really have, then give them to me." This is as true for people as it is for bread and fish. We may think we have little to offer, or that we ourselves don't amount to much. Jesus and Zephaniah tell us differently. They show us that God takes what is small and of little significance in the world's eyes and creates overflowing abundance. The Lord God who spoke the universe into existence can certainly do a lot with a little.

Three times Zephaniah tells us how crucial it is for us to "seek the LORD." In even stronger terms, we are to "pursue him" (Zephaniah 1:6, 2:3, 3:12). In Hebrew, pursue means to run after. Seek means to search out, to strive after, to desire, to require. Do we run after God? Do we require God's presence as if our very lives depend upon it? If so, we do not have to run far because, as Zephaniah promises us, "the LORD your God is in your midst" (3:17).

Prophetic Back to Basics

Nahum, Habakkuk, and Zephaniah saw and heard things from God that the average person does not. That's what prophecy is all about. Even so, their messages are not full of radical surprises. God is still the great "I Am Who I Am" (Exodus 3:14) who says, "I am the LORD, and I do not change" (Malachi 3:6). The prophets plainly tell us once again to get our houses in order and remember to whom we owe our lives. In various ways and circumstances, they all agree with Micah: God has told us what is good and what is required of us (Micah 6:8). Nations come and go. People are faithful or not, but the basics of a righteous life have been clear from the beginning.

In Jeremiah 9:22-23, God declares the basics once again:

Let not the wise man glory in his wisdom;
Let not the strong man glory in his strength;
Let not the rich man glory in his riches.
But only in this should one glory:
In his earnest devotion to Me.
For I the LORD act with kindness,
Justice, and equity in the world;
For in these I delight
                              —declares the LORD.[4]

All the prophets say that our hope lies in earnest devotion to God. Jesus puts it this way: "Desire first and foremost God's kingdom and God's righteousness" (Matthew 6:33). How do we foster this devotion? Nahum,

Habakkuk, and Zephaniah offer some practical attitudes and habits that bring us closer to God and build our hope:

- We are humble, not proud. Our only boast is in knowing God.
- God receives our greatest love and highest loyalty. Nothing or anyone comes before the Lord.
- We obey God and do not rationalize what is clearly wrong or nonsensical. We are sure that God's will and God's way are always in our best interest.
- We talk freely to God, confessing our sins, expressing our doubts, bringing our fears out in the open.
- We listen for God to speak through the Word and the Spirit. Like the prophets, we wait patiently and expectantly for guidance. Hope does not come from our own wisdom or power. Hope comes from God.
- "Come hell or high water," we respect God and trust God's purposes. God is at work in the world and in our lives, both in the big picture and the small details.

Nahum, Habakkuk, and Zephaniah show us how active God is in the world and how available God is to everyone. Those who ardently seek God will not be disappointed. The prophets also expect God to take care of our physical needs. They picture God's redeemed people living in safety and enjoying the fruits of their labors.

The prophets are abundantly clear about the consequences of sinful, unrighteous living. Their hope is clear, too. They see the way to life and peace with God, and they know we each have choices to make. Do we choose to pursue God and the hope God offers?

Live the Story

The blues is a distinctive musical style that came out of the rural Deep South, particularly the Mississippi Delta. Born out of hard times and the experiences of slaves, sharecroppers, and the poor, the blues tell stories of poverty, love, oppression, the foibles of human nature, and even faith. Blues melodies, with their flattened third, fifth, and seventh chords, carry these stories to emotional heights and depths beyond speech alone.

"Singing the blues" gives voice to our heartaches and hardships, and then often helps us move on in spite of them.

Legendary bluesman B. B. King, often hailed as "King of the Blues," was born on a Mississippi cotton plantation. Now a composer, singer, and guitarist, King once plowed fields and picked cotton as a youth. He knows how to "Let the Good Times Roll," and he also knows how alone we all can feel at times. In "Nobody Loves Me But My Mother," he gets to the heart of loneliness and doubt: "Nobody loves me but my mother, and she could be jivin' too. Now you see why I act funny, baby, when you do the things you do."[5]

Sometimes it seems like even God is jivin' us. With no relief in sight, hope can appear like a facetious promise. And with no hope, we surely can act funny, or worse.

Nahum, Habakkuk, and Zephaniah declare that hope is real and that it is for us. God is not jivin' anyone. One modern affirmation of faith says, "We believe in God the Father, / infinite in wisdom, power, and love, / whose mercy is over all his works, / and whose will is ever directed to his children's good."[6] The prophets reassure us that God does work for our good. We may find this hard to believe when we feel like lonely castoffs. However, when we stand watch and wait for a word from God, we can truly expect good news.

1. From *http://www.georgiaencyclopedia.org/nge/Article.jsp?id=h-977*. Also see *http://www.ajc.com/news/lifestyles/resurrection-of-finsters-paradise-garden/nQTP8/*.
2. From *The Prophets: The New JPS Translation of the Holy Scriptures According to the Traditional Hebrew Text* (The Jewish Publication Society of America, 1978); page 857.
3. From *http://www.georgiaencyclopedia.org/nge/Article.jsp?id=h-977*.
4. From *The Prophets*; page 541.
5. Lyrics by B.B. King, © Universal Music Publishing Group, EMI Music Publishing.
6. From "A Modern Affirmation," in *The United Methodist Hymnal* (The United Methodist Publishing House, 1989); 885.

5.

Haggai and Zechariah: Confronting Situational Blindness

Haggai and Zechariah

Claim Your Story

We all love shortcuts. Saving time is a major obsession in our culture, and speed is prized. We don't often hear the admonition "Stop and think." Instead, we rely on habit, well-known rules of thumb, or our electronic gadgets to save us time and mental effort.

However, always following well-worn paths in our thinking can get us into trouble. It can lead to what is called situational blindness. This means that we rely on preconceived ideas and disregard what's actually happening around us. Situational blindness causes us to ignore vital information that can help us make good decisions. We focus on what we think *should* be happening instead of what *is* happening. This leads to unfounded assumptions about what will happen next and about the choices we need to make.

For example, we may drive without focusing on a familiar road because we are engrossed in a phone conversation and just assume the journey will always be safe. We might persist in following GPS directions into a dead end despite the fact that our surroundings don't match our expectations. We could also be so set in our orientation that, against reason, we convince ourselves that water does indeed flow uphill, and so we follow a stream away from our downhill destination instead of toward it.

An antidote to situational blindness is what's called situational awareness. This simply means that we take the time to check our environment to see what it is telling us. We ask ourselves, "What's happening now?" and "What's about to happen?" This mental discipline is used by fighter pilots in what is called the OODA loop. They *observe, orient, decide,* and *act* in a continuing thought process so they perform well and survive against enemy pilots.[1]

As prophets, Haggai and Zechariah had to confront situational blindness of both mind and spirit. God's people were back in Jerusalem after decades of exile in Babylon, but they were wasting this blessed opportunity. Given the chance to rebuild their city and their lives under God's direction, they struggled and were too blind to see why things were not going well.

In response, the prophets offered them a way to observe, orient, decide, and act as God wanted them to act. Haggai said, "Take your ways to heart" (1:5), and be realistic about how things are going and where you are headed. Zechariah affirmed what other prophets had been saying for generations: Only by God's Spirit do we survive and thrive, and we must listen to God's word.

Enter the Bible Story

A Difficult Homecoming

Sometimes getting what we want is not what we hoped it would be. Exiled Israelites who joyfully returned to Jerusalem from Babylon immediately saw what they were up against. The Persians, their new masters, willingly let them go with the expectation that worship in the Temple would resume. It was a very pragmatic move for the Persian overlords. Giving subject peoples some autonomy and religious freedom tends to keep them less restless and rebellious. King Cyrus gave specific permission for the Temple to be rebuilt and even allowed the return of looted Temple treasure (Ezra 6:3-12).

It wouldn't be like the old days when the Jews had a king in the line of David on the throne and had complete independence, but it was still a welcome turn of events. The Israelites had longed for home, and now they could go. When they finally did go back to Jerusalem, however, life was hard. Some fifty years after Jerusalem's destruction by the Babylonians, it was still mostly in ruins. The city and its population were small compared to pre-exilic times. There were few people and resources to renew and rebuild. Jerusalem's protective wall was broken down and wouldn't be fully repaired until Nehemiah's return almost one hundred years later (Nehemiah 1–7).

The Israelites who stayed in Judah were eking out a living in a plundered land. Though their masters had changed, they were still under foreign domination and were harassed by neighboring peoples who now claimed former Judean territory. There were also tensions between the Israelites and the Samaritans in the former Kingdom of Israel to the north. Samaritans were a blend of native Jews and immigrants from around the Assyrian empire. Though the Jews of Samaria and Judah were ancient kinsmen, they had different styles of worship and ways of following God. The tensions and mistrust between them endured into Jesus' time (John 4:1-42).

Not surprisingly, there were also tensions between those who returned and those who had stayed in Judah, including questions about the ownership of ancestral property. The purity of worship in Jerusalem had also been compromised with the loss of the Temple and the pervasive influence of pagan cults.

The exiles returned with official sanction to rebuild the Temple, and leaders rallied people to the task, but progress was short-lived. They rebuilt the altar and repaired the foundation (Ezra 3; 5:16), but their main focus was on their own homes. They were like some of the soil in Jesus' parable of the sower (Mark 4:1-20). They heard God's word (the seed) and took it into their hearts (the soil), but the seed produced no fruit because it was choked out by thorny plants (worry and greed). Haggai and Zechariah found that the hearts of God's people in Jerusalem had been thorny ground for the past twenty years. The people knew that sin and disobedience brought war, exile, and ruin to their nation. They also knew that God still desired a faithful relationship with God's chosen people. Even so, the cares of everyday life and the thorns of adversity were choking out the good word the prophets had sown into their lives. They were giving half-hearted, inconsistent effort toward their God-given responsibilities. God's word did not flourish in their hearts or spur them to consistent good works.

Zechariah put the situation succinctly: Judah was once "a delightful land," but it was now "a wasteland" (7:14). The saving grace is that God does some of his best work in the wilderness, in the "wastelands" of our lives and circumstances.

About the Scripture

Faithful in Foreign Lands

The *Diaspora* is the name for Jews who were "scattered abroad," living outside of Judah after 587 b.c. With the destruction of Jerusalem, some fled to Egypt and others were exiled to Babylon. Many Jews never returned to Judah, and they followed Jeremiah's word to flourish in exile and not "dwindle away" (Jeremiah 29:6). They settled, raised families, worked, prospered, and lived out their faith in these new lands. Their communities became fertile ground for growing their faith and traditions. The Temple had been the center of sacrifice and study and the epicenter of God's presence in the Promised Land. Away from the Temple and the land, they still studied Torah, and they recorded what had previously been mostly oral law and tradition about their faith.

The Egyptian Diaspora produced the Septuagint, a Greek translation of the Hebrew Old Testament. By the third century b.c., most of their community could no longer speak or read Hebrew, and they needed Scriptures in their new native tongue. Today the Septuagint is a great resource for biblical scholars. It gives us a glimpse into the ancient Hebrew manuscripts that were used for the Greek translation and that are no longer available for study in the original.

The Babylonian Diaspora flourished for hundreds of years. They set up academies that were centers for scholarship and the development of Jewish law. These academies produced what is now called the Babylonian Talmud. This is a 2,711-page record of teaching, study, and learning among the rabbis in Babylon. Over many generations they recorded their conversations and debates about the laws, ethics, customs, and theology that governed Jewish life. The Babylonian Talmud is written in Aramaic, the common language of Persia, with quotes from Hebrew Scripture. Orthodox Jews worldwide still study this Talmud in a seven-and-a-half-year cycle, reading one page a day with everyone on the same page each day.

In Psalm 137:4, an exile asks a poignant question, "How could we possibly sing the LORD's song on foreign soil?" The Diaspora found an answer to this question. They figured out how to "sing" through the preservation of Scripture and the dedicated study and practice of God's Word.

The Men and the Mission

Haggai is simply identified as "the prophet" (1:1), the one who was called to speak for God. He may have lived in exile before returning to Jerusalem sometime between 538–520 B.C. His prophecies are dated from mid-August/mid-September until mid-November/mid-December of 520 B.C. Zechariah was from a priestly family and also returned to Jerusalem from exile. Some of his prophecies are dated to mid-October/mid-November of 520 B.C. (1:1), to mid-January /mid-February of 519 B.C. (1:7), and to mid-November/mid-December of 519 B.C. (7:1). Haggai's and Zechariah's prophetic ministries kept the pressure on the Israelite community in Jerusalem to finish the Temple and resume proper worship.

They specifically addressed Zerubbabel, who was appointed governor of Judah by the Persians, and Joshua, the high priest. The prophets knew that both civil and religious leadership were needed to get the job done. Three weeks after Haggai's first word from the Lord was proclaimed to the people, work restarted on the Lord's house. Haggai's and Zechariah's passionate messages were crucial to the completion and rededication of the Temple, which was celebrated in the spring of 515 B.C.

Both Haggai and Zechariah were prophets with priestly concerns for the Temple and for the sanctity of God's people. They knew that the Temple was God's dwelling within the community of faith, and its rituals gave order to its life. The Temple was also the vital focal point for the community to make a new start as God's chosen people in the Promised Land. It was a tangible expression of their loyalty to and faith in God, which was something they all still had in common after so many years of being separated.

Before the exile, Jeremiah said,

> The LORD proclaims:
> Stop at the crossroads and look around;
>   ask for the ancient paths.
>   Where is the good way?
> Then walk in it
>   and find a resting place for yourselves. (Jeremiah 6:16)

Haggai and Zechariah found the Israelites at yet another crossroads. These prophets were sent by God to remind everyone where the ancient paths were and how to choose the good way. It is obvious that the people were going down the wrong road, but they were just not seeing it. Haggai and Zechariah were there to give them a clear-eyed view of what was happening and what was at stake.

We all can struggle, barely get by, and flounder spiritually when we lose our focus. It is a persistent part of our human condition. Jesus saw this, too, and shows us how to put first things first:

Therefore, don't worry and say, "What are we going to eat?" or "What are we going to drink?" or "What are we going to wear?" . . . Your heavenly Father knows that you need them. Instead, desire first and foremost God's kingdom and God's righteousness, and all these things will be given to you as well. Therefore, stop worrying about tomorrow, because tomorrow will worry about itself. Each day has enough trouble of its own. (Matthew 6:31-34)

Prophetic Reality Check

For almost twenty years, God's chosen people had been focusing on the wrong things. Rebuilding the Temple was supposed to be their primary mission. Instead they procrastinated, saying, "The time hasn't come, the time to rebuild the LORD's house" (Haggai 1:2). They devoted their energies to their own houses, which were not just make-do dwellings. They built "paneled" or "cieled" (KJV) houses for themselves (Haggai 1:4), making sure they had sound roofs over their heads. Meanwhile, God's house was exposed to the elements and lay in ruins. God was paying attention to all this and quoted their disobedient words back to them, letting them know how God saw them. Instead of seeing a faithful, worshipping community, God saw a people of unclean hearts and actions (Haggai 2:14). It wasn't a pretty picture. The Temple was in shambles. Their economy was struggling, and they worked hard for very little gain. Natural calamities affected their crops and livestock (Haggai 1:6-11; 2:15-17). After twenty years of effort, they were still living in a wasteland.

Repeatedly Haggai says, "Take your ways to heart" (1:5, 7) and "take it to heart" (2:15, 18). Other translations say, "Consider how you have been faring!"[2] and "Consider your ways *and* set your mind on what has come to you" (AMP). In other words, let's practice some situational awareness! In Hebrew, *heart* represents the whole person. It is the center of physical vitality and also the source of emotion, thought, reflection, and intellect. The biblical "heart" is also intimately connected to the will. It is the core out of which we make decisions and the means by which we choose obedience and devotion to God. Jesus also had a lot to say about our hearts. (See, for example, Matthew 5:8, 28; Mark 6:52; 7:6-7.) Our hearts show who we are and what we value. Haggai was not asking his people for a superficial look around. He was demanding an honest assessment of reality and a fundamental change of heart.

Taking a clear, unbiased look at our lives can be unpleasant. The momentum of habit and the rush of life can also carry us along to someplace we never really planned to go. Just forcing ourselves to stop and look at how we are truly faring takes time and courage. Situational blindness is all too easy, and facing reality can be hard.

Sometimes others, including the prophets, can see us more clearly than we can see ourselves. In a *Far Side* cartoon, two bears are standing at the edge of a forest watching oversized, naked humans at a nudist colony. One bear says to the other, "Well, there goes *my* appetite."[3] We might say the same thing about ourselves if we take the prophet's instruction to heart. Even so, Haggai and Zechariah tell us that it is absolutely necessary to face the unadorned truth. Lamentations 3:40 puts it this way: "We must search and examine our ways; / we must return to the LORD."

Taking Our Ways to Heart

What do the prophets tell us about taking stock of ourselves and living with good situational awareness? They tell us that we are to accept that God is not a disinterested bystander in our lives. God always pays attention to our obedience and our fruitfulness. God sends his word, and it is up to us to keep our hearts as fertile soil for the word to grow and flourish. If we are willing, God gives us hearts to know him (Jeremiah 24:7) and the power to discern God's will.

The prophets affirm that God has specific purposes for God's people to fulfill in this world. These purposes are linked to God's larger purposes for creation. The Jews who labored to rebuild the Temple after the exile certainly benefitted from the labor and the worship that followed. They also were working for the thousands of people who came after them, the people of many nations drawn to this special place of God's presence on earth.

Haggai and Zechariah are also not going to let anyone get away with whining or making excuses. It's a waste of time to tell them that a God-given task is too hard. Zechariah says, "Be strong," because God always provides strength and courage for the task at hand. The prophets say unequivocally to fear God, not our circumstances.

Haggai and Zechariah, like all the prophets, listened to God and put obedience first on their to-do lists. Rushing or plodding through life out of habit keeps our focus too narrow. Fear can blind us to a better way. Wisdom is available if we will take an honest look at our hearts and our situations.

Haggai and Zechariah tell us that change is both possible and necessary. We remember God's goodness and then let go of the past and move ahead.

Live the Story

The Palace of Holyroodhouse in Edinburgh, Scotland, is an official residence of the British monarch. On the palace grounds are the ruins of a twelfth-century abbey, which are soaring testimony to faith in God and also haunting evidence of a violent past. A wall of the abbey holds an epitaph for Thomas Lowes, who died in 1812 at age 61. The inscription honors Lowes's memory and also offers a lesson for the living. It says that Lowes enjoyed great success and many possessions, lost it all, gained it back, and then died. Further, we are told that his life is "one instance among thousands of the uncertainty of human life, and the instability of earthly possessions and enjoyments. . . . Reader, be thou taught by this, to seek those riches which never can fail, and those pleasures which are at God's right hand forevermore, the gracious gift of God, and to be enjoyed through faith in Jesus Christ, our Savior."[4]

Much of what we dedicate ourselves to is temporary and does not last beyond our lifetimes. Even the Temple that God asked the Israelites to rebuild at great effort did not stand forever. In the end this Temple, like the one before it, was destroyed. So what is the point? Haggai and Zechariah tell us that the work of rebuilding and the Temple itself are a means to an end. Knowing and trusting God are the only sure and eternal things. God asks us to put our hearts and souls into trusting him and into the work God gives us to do. Then, we turn it all over to God to do with as God pleases. Our part is to trust, listen, and obey. We keep our hearts oriented to God's ways and choose God's purposes over our own. In this, Haggai and Zechariah tell us, we find "those riches which never can fail."

1. For more information, read "Deadly Mind Traps," by Jeff Wise, in *Psychology Today* (January 1, 2012); *http://www.psychologytoday.com/articles/201112/deadly-mind-traps*.
2. From *The Prophets: The New JPS Translation of the Holy Scriptures According to the Traditional Hebrew Text* (The Jewish Publication Society of America, 1978); page 869.
3. From *The Far Side*, by Gary Larson (FarWorks, Inc., Universal Press Syndicate, 1988).
4. From *A Popular Description of St. Paul's Cathedral*, Seventeenth Edition, by Maria Hackett (J.B. Nichols and Son, 1828); page 53.

6.

Haggai and Zechariah: Profound Possibilities

Haggai and Zechariah

Claim Your Story

The word *Imagineering*, which is a combination of "imagination" and "engineering," is familiar to anyone who has visited one of the Walt Disney Company theme parks. Disney uses this term to describe the skills and artistry it takes to develop its vast array of entertainment projects.

Tackling some of the more mundane aspects of daily life, such as traffic congestion, often takes a similar combination of imagination and engineering. For those of us with limited imaginations and no engineering skills, the solution to relieving congestion might just be wider roads and more traffic signals. Fortunately, people with livelier imaginations and greater knowledge have come up with what is called a "diverging diamond" traffic pattern to help keep traffic moving. This is a relatively quick and inexpensive solution for congestion in situations where left turns across heavy traffic are causing big backups.

The key to a diverging diamond is sending traffic in both directions from the right lanes into the left lanes for a short distance and then back into the right lanes again, all without adding bridges or underpasses. It uses strategically placed lane markers, islands, and signals to keep traffic flowing safely. How such a scheme actually works might be hard for many of us to visualize. Fortunately again, people with great imaginations and practical skills have produced a computer-generated fly-over of a working diverging diamond intersection (see the video link at the bottom of page 67).[1] Seeing the video produces an "Oh, I see it now!" moment. It then makes perfect sense, and you are ready to navigate such an intersection in real life without wondering what in the world you are getting yourself into.

We obviously don't get instructional videos from the prophets, just powerful words. Instead of calling on imagination and engineering, Haggai's and Zechariah's messages demand our faith, devotion, and willingness to see things in a new light from God's point of view. The prophets are certainly concerned about practical, everyday life, and they have much to say about how we go about our business, family, and religious lives. They also push us to look beyond what we can physically see and touch. While Imagineering can be both fun and useful, Haggai and Zechariah show us a greater reality. They ask us to allow for profound, life-changing possibilities when the Lord of heavenly forces is in our midst and in our hearts.

Enter the Bible Story

Though Haggai is identified simply as "the prophet" (1:1), his messages combine prophetic concern for faithful and ethical living with priestly concern for the Temple and worship. Zechariah also was a prophet with priestly concerns. He was dedicated to seeing the Temple rebuilt and its rituals restored along with upholding justice and righteousness within the community. Zechariah was well-versed in the Law and Temple procedures and helped his people navigate the intricacies of keeping the covenant and worshiping God properly. He was also a visionary who saw how God was working behind the scenes to usher in a new era of peace and spiritual harmony. Zechariah's concern for our daily walk of faith is intimately connected to a more exalted and sweeping reality.

The Lord of Heavenly Forces

Haggai's and Zechariah's immediate concerns were for the Temple and the faithfulness of God's people in Jerusalem. They knew that the Temple

About the Scripture

Heavenly Forces at Work in the World

Both Haggai and Zechariah call God the "Lord of hosts" (NRSV) or the "Lord of heavenly forces" (CEB) over and over again. This name for God is found 279 times in the Old Testament, most often in the prophets. Haggai uses it fourteen times in just two chapters, and Zechariah uses it fifty-two times in fourteen chapters. There is no doubt that the God for whom they speak is not some petty, man-made local deity. Their God is the supreme commander of all creation, which includes the invisible as well as the visible realm. Zechariah speaks with an "angel" (NRSV) or "messenger" (CEB) who helps him understand his visions and who explains their meanings.

Throughout Scripture, heavenly beings provide knowledge and insight for prophets and others (for example, Genesis 21:17-21; Luke 1:26-38). Jesus said that the Son of Man has angels at his command who will participate in the judgment at the end of the present age (Matthew 13:41; 2 Thessalonians 1:7).

was a unique point of contact for God and the community of faith. They also knew that this human structure, no matter how special it was, could not completely contain God. The Lord would not just settle into the nice new Holy of Holies and wait for people to come pay him homage. From the beginning, the Lord has been active in creation and human history and has multitudes of heavenly beings to help accomplish God's purposes in heaven and on earth.

The Lord of hosts also seeks human beings to help accomplish God's purposes: the famous and the unknown, prophets, kings, judges, laborers, warriors, those who are faithful and even those whose faith is sometimes in doubt. The Lord and the prophets have no illusions about any of us. They know what we are thinking, saying, feeling, and doing. Nevertheless, both then and now, God's grand purposes are fostered by limited, ordinary people. Haggai and Zechariah tell us that even small and temporal things really do matter in the eternal scheme of things. For the people of Jerusalem, rebuilding the Temple and treating one another with kindness and justice were straightforward and familiar commands. There are no big surprises here, just the expectation that they get on with the business at hand, with what they know is right and good.

Haggai plainly calls people to examine their hearts, minds, and circumstances. Be honest about yourselves, he says, and face up to what your unfaithfulness has caused. Zechariah then opens with a call to repentance. Through the prophet, God tells his people that they have walked out on their relationship with God. In contrast, their stubborn ancestors had the courage to admit that they brought the exile on themselves and to repent. Those who were blessed with a new beginning in Jerusalem needed to do the same. Repentance, which brings a clean heart and fresh start with God, comes first. A renewed relationship with God opens the door to insight and hope for the future. It brings the ability to see reality in a new dimension and to see God's hand at work in the world. This, Zechariah says in his visions, is what is going on. He fully expected the people to live faithfully under the Law while remaining open to God's actions beyond their limited view.

Seeing the big picture, especially God's big picture, takes an open spirit and dedicated effort. In the physical world, a good parallel to this is what is known as the Sanibel Stoop. The beaches of Sanibel and Captiva Islands on the Gulf Coast of Florida are paradise for seashell collectors. There are so many incredible shells for the taking that people literally can hardly take their eyes off the sand, and so they walk for miles in that peculiar posture called the Sanibel Stoop. Looking up and away from what is under their feet would reveal beautiful views of sky and water. But the stoop and its narrow focus win out with most beach-goers. Likewise, we can have a hard time drawing our spiritual eyes away from our visible, everyday joys and concerns. This is especially challenging when prophetic visions of God's invisible realm are strange to us, and we just don't understand what meaning we are to take from them. The details may baffle us, but at the very least, we can affirm our trust in God's ultimate purposes for us and for the world.

Zechariah's Night Visions

Law, Temple, and vision were all important to the community of faith. In Zechariah's first vision (1:8-17), angelic messengers and horsemen tell the prophet that the seventy years of Israel's punishment that were declared by Jeremiah (Jeremiah 25:11) are over. Though the nations of the world may be at rest, they have overstepped their bounds of violence and will face God's anger. God is returning to Jerusalem with passion and compassion for her future.

The second vision (Zechariah 1:18-21) tells that the power ("horns") of these other nations will be destroyed by metalworkers who dismantle their weapons of tyranny.

The third vision (2:1-13) proclaims that measuring tools are unnecessary for the new Jerusalem because the Lord will be its protecting wall and its glory within. God confirms the destruction of the plundering nations and the return of Israel's exiles to Zion. Israel is precious (the "pupil" or "apple" of God's eye, verse 8), but the glories of Zion and God's presence are for other nations, too. All will rejoice and then be moved to awed silence as God claims them as God's own.

In the fourth night vision (3:1-10), the high priest Joshua represents all of Israel. He and God's people are guilty of sin but are now forgiven, cleansed, and renewed.

The fifth vision (4:1-14) focuses on Zerubbabel, the governor of Judah, who would see that the Temple was rebuilt. The lamps fueled by olive oil symbolize God's anointed leaders, Zerubbabel and Joshua. Previous struggles ("a time of little things," verse 10) will give way to rejoicing as God's Spirit brings true power and strength to the task at hand.

In the sixth vision (5:1-4), a flying scroll symbolizes God's word as it seeks out and punishes sin. This includes sins against people in the community ("stealing," verse 3) and against God ("swearing lies," verse 3).

The seventh vision (5:5-11) pictures wickedness and idol worship leaving Jerusalem and being carried to a temple in Babylon. Idol worship has no place in God's city or among God's chosen people.

The eighth vision (6:1-8) again brings angelic messengers who patrol the earth. Babylon ("the north country," verse 6) is subdued, and God's Spirit is at rest concerning them. God's purposes for the earth and for Israel in particular are being accomplished.

Zechariah's visions reveal the progression of God's plans for Israel. Exile and repentance set the stage for the return to Jerusalem. God comes with God's people to bring peace, cleansing, forgiveness, purity, and right-eousness. God is prepared to dwell in Jerusalem and to draw all peoples into the fold of a faithful worshiping community.

Zechariah's Day of the Lord

Zechariah 9–14 also contains prophetic pronouncements about the future. These chapters are sometimes called Second Zechariah because some scholars believe they are from later disciples of the prophet at the end of the fourth and beginning of the third centuries B.C. Regardless of the time frame, these prophecies reflect the fact that wars and political instability continued even after the Temple was rebuilt and rededicated. Leaders in Israel also consistently failed to hold a high standard of faithfulness and justice within the community. These last visions speak of a time when God brings sweeping change to the world at large through the power of a humble king, a messiah in the line of David.

First, God moves against Israel's enemies (9:1-8) and even brings the hated Philistines into the faithful community. This sets the stage for a new king, who rides on a donkey instead of a warhorse and who speaks peace instead of violence (9:9-10). This king is in right standing with God and vanquishes God's enemies. He is also humble and understands the suffering and afflictions experienced by God's people.

The Lord of heavenly forces engages the forces that threaten God's people (9:11-17). The exiles, who have been "prisoners of hope" (verse 12), return to the Promised Land to be paid back double for what they have lost. No longer pawns in the hands of foreign powers, the people sparkle and flourish under God's gracious deliverance.

God is the Lord of creation who takes care of the chosen people ("his splendor," 10:3). False prophets and unreliable leaders within the community as well as external enemies will not stand in the way of God's plans for return and renewal. No longer going astray or living in exile, God's people truly walk in God's strength and God's way.

Before complete renewal can happen, however, towering pride and rampant injustice must be confronted (11:1-17). Magnificent cedars and oaks represent human arrogance that falls before God's cleansing wrath.

Shepherds who devour their flocks instead of protecting them are Israel's leaders who again fail in their God-given responsibilities. The prophet acts out the broken covenant by chopping up the shepherd's staff of "Delight" (verse 10) and then chops up the staff of "Harmony" (verse 14) to show the broken kinship between Israel and Judah. The sinful, foolish shepherds are doomed.

The last three chapters of Zechariah look ahead to an all-encompassing time of judgment and redemption for God's people. After all these years and all that the prophets have said on God's behalf, the community of faith is still broken and sinful. "On that day," the day of great power that belongs to the Lord, sin and oppression will fall both inside and outside the community of faith.

First come assurances that Judah and Jerusalem will survive the assaults of other nations (12:1-9). Israel herself must be cleansed and redeemed from sin, however. For the community to be renewed, a godly leader dies a sacrificial death that opens a cleansing fountain, washing away sin and impurity (12:9–13:1). Idols are banished, and false prophets who bring a "sinful spirit" (13:2) to the community will be ashamed and cease their deceptions (13:6). God's chosen shepherd dies, as does two thirds of the community. The surviving remnant endures a crucible of refinement so they can truly say, "The LORD is our God" (13:7-9).

The climactic day of the Lord brings violence and terror to Jerusalem, its people, and the land itself before redemption and peace reign (14:1-21). All these cataclysmic images paint a picture of the day of the Lord that is disturbing and disorienting. But Zechariah is leading us to a very different picture at the end of that day: Finally, peace reigns and even the bells of horses testify to the holiness that now graces Jerusalem. Common pots are holy and consecrated for sacrificial service in the Temple. The people and their pots are clean after being impure (Haggai 2:10-14). People of all nations come to worship in peace and harmony.

In the meantime, Haggai says that Zerubbabel has a special role to play in God's plans for Israel (Haggai 2:20-23). He serves in the line of David and prefigures the Messiah, who will bring ultimate deliverance. Zechariah makes a crown for Joshua the High Priest (Zechariah 6:9-15) and one for a king who will come later. The two leaders will one day lead the people in peace if the people are obedient and listen to God's instruction. The prophet also deals with questions about ritual fasting and lamentation (7:1-13). Zechariah's answer goes beyond the ritual to the attitudes behind it. He asks, "Were your hearts in it? Or was it merely self-justifying formality?" Like all his fellow prophets, Zechariah declares that formalities can never take the place of justice, kindness, and compassion.

Hope for God's People

Through Zechariah, God asked "the remnant" (8:12) of Israel to be strong, faithful, and expectant (8:1-23). Though they were small in number and scope, God chose once again to dwell in their midst. Divine anger against sin gives way to gracious and forgiving love toward those who truly seek God. Great joy and peace are indeed possible! Jerusalem gains new life as "the city of truth" (8:3). People of all nations know that God is there and are drawn to God's presence on the holy mount. The land and the people flourish in material and spiritual abundance, and those who were once cursed are now blessed beyond measure. Strength, not fear, characterizes God's people. Fear has no place in their hearts because God declares, "They will be my people, and I will be their God—in truth and in righteousness" (8:8). Whether or not we understand all the details, this promise is for us, too.

Live the Story

The world is still a fearful place, and much of the time fear comes easier to us than strength. We see that the prophets' promises of total redemption and renewal are works in progress. They are in progress for sure, but fulfillment seems out of reach right now. We may say with confidence that God does have the last word, but sometimes we can't hear that word for all the racket of sin and uncertainty in our lives. Sin, worry, and our perpetual busy-ness cloud our spirits and darken our vision for what God is doing just out of easy sight. Thankfully, the truth does shine through at times, and we get a glimpse of what God's redeemed world might look like.

Michael Arad is the architect who designed the 9/11 memorial in New York City, which honors the people who died at the World Trade Center site in the terrorist attacks on September 11, 2001. Arad is a native of Israel and had lived in New York City only two and a half years before that horrific day. He says, "It changed who I am. I became a New Yorker, because of what happened here." His memorial design, called Reflecting Absence, includes waterfalls that flow into voids where the twin towers once stood. Bronze parapets surround the waterfalls and contain the names of those who died that day and those who died in the attack on the World Trade Center in February 1993.

To arrange the names on the parapets, the design team consulted family members of those who were killed. The result is what Arad calls "meaningful adjacency," in which the names of certain people who knew one another are placed next to or near one another. Almost 2,700 people perished at what is now called Ground Zero, people from many nations, backgrounds, and faiths. Millions of people from many nations have visited the memorial to pay their respects and to remember the lives lost.[2]

If people from around the world can live, work, remember, and grieve together, there is hope that one day we can live in harmony and joy and faith together. The prophets are clear that we cannot do this by our own merit or strength. It is only by God's power and grace that we, like those simple bells and common pots, can be transformed for holy service. We trust, watch, and serve. When God's great day of redemption comes, we will be ready, "neither by power, nor by strength, / but by my spirit, says the LORD of heavenly forces" (Zechariah 4:6).

---

1. Watch the video at *http://www.youtube.com/watch?v=gY8xU-UAQWs*.
2. From *http://news.yahoo.com/blogs/newsmakers/9-11-memorial-offers-quiet-amid-new-york-chaos-designer-michael-arad-says.html*.

7.

Malachi: Calling for a Spiritual Makeover

Malachi

Claim Your Story

In recent years, the reality show genre has proliferated on television. The pioneer of such programs was *Candid Camera*, which began as a radio broadcast called *Candid Microphone* in 1947 and, starting in 1948, aired original television shows for decades.[1] In the so-called reality of the show, confounding or practical-joke situations were arranged for unsuspecting participants to encounter, and the unfolding "comedy" was filmed by hidden cameras. Listening to and watching people get flustered and confused proved to be very popular, though it was probably less funny to those on the receiving end of the pranks.

A recent show of the reality genre is *What Not to Wear*, which coaches a fashion-challenged individual in developing a more attractive style of dress, make-up, and hair. Most participants are nominated for the show by friends or family members who despair of this person's current looks. Once nominated for a makeover, the sartorially deficient person is secretly filmed, which graphically reveals their unkempt and/or unstylish appearance. Watching the hidden camera footage is most always an unpleasant, "gotcha" experience for the nominee.[2]

Many, if not most, of us would probably not look too great either if we were subjected to the same scrutiny. It's also hard to cope gracefully with a situation designed to make us look silly, and it's even worse to have it filmed for the entire world to see. The worst "gotcha," however, might well be to have a video of all that we say and do during a typical day. This would lead to some serious questions, not about how we dress or how flustered we get if we are the butt of a joke, but about our character and our faith. Are our actions always honorable and our speech pleasing to God?

Instead of television crews with hidden cameras and microphones following us around, Malachi says that it's God who is watching and listening. For the people of Israel, the results were not remotely laudable. A playback of our own daily lives could also be much more revealing and far less flattering than any reality show set-up. God does not set us up to be confused or play jokes on us, but God's prophets are not reticent about revealing our shortcomings. When we are in need of a spiritual makeover, they are just the ones to do it.

Enter the Bible Story

Malachi (whose name in Hebrew means "my messenger") began his prophetic ministry not long after Haggai and Zechariah. The biblical book bearing his name includes no biographical information. He was simply the one called to bear the burden of God's message and to lift these words up to his people. With Haggai's and Zechariah's leadership, the Temple was finished and rededicated for worship in 515 B.C. This was supposed to serve as a catalyst and focal point for the rededication of the community as well. Their identity as God's chosen people was shaky, and they desperately needed to renew their covenant vows of faithfulness to God and fidelity to one another. As is often the case, however, rebuilding stone and wood is easier than rebuilding hearts and lives. It's "déjà vu all over again" with corruption and immorality among the people and even within the Temple itself. The paint was hardly dry before priests were offering second-rate sacrifices and men were divorcing their Israelite wives to marry pagans and worship false gods.

In a series of six prophetic disputes, Malachi revealed God's close attention to what the people and their priests were saying and doing. These disputes are conversations between God and the people. Both God and the people ask questions, and God answers. Malachi leaves no doubt about who has the truth and who has the last word, no matter what the issue is. Like Haggai and Zechariah, Malachi repeatedly calls God the "LORD of heavenly forces." He uses this name twenty-four times, repeating the obvious because he knew how hard-headed and spiritually deaf people can be. "Listen," he says. "You are untrue to the one true God, the one who has heavenly warriors and all creation at his command." In other words, "Are you crazy? Look who you are dealing with!" God's power is all-encompassing and so is God's knowledge. The conversational style of Malachi's prophecies shows that the Lord of heavenly forces is very much up close and personal, too.

Across the Testaments

There's No Hiding From God

It should surprise no one that God is listening, watching, and cares about what is going on in the world. Genesis tells us that Adam and Eve walked and talked with God in the garden of Eden, and God went looking for them when they tried to hide their sin and shame (Genesis 3). The Torah (Genesis through Deuteronomy) repeatedly shows that God did not just give the Law and then walk away. God set the covenant boundaries and controlled the consequences of faithfulness and of disobedience (Deuteronomy 28). Israel's history is full of instances when God took an active role on a national level and in individual lives. The prophet Nathan exposed David's sin with Bathsheba and in her husband Uriah's death (2 Samuel 12:1-15). In 2 Chronicles 16:9, Hanani the seer tells King Asa of Judah that "the LORD's eyes scan the whole world to strengthen those who are committed to him with all their hearts."

Old Testament prophets say again and again that God is right here, right now, watching, listening, and instructing. Some two hundred years before Malachi, Micah quoted community leaders who were telling prophets not to preach and who wanted to silence these messages from God (Micah 2:6-11). Malachi clearly shows that what people say at home, in the streets, in court, and in the Temple is noticed and noted by God.

The New Testament is likewise clear that Jesus knows what people are thinking and what they are saying. For example, when legal experts were offended that Jesus was bold enough to declare someone's sins forgiven, "Jesus knew what they were thinking and said, 'Why do you fill your minds with evil things?'" (Matthew 9:4; see also Matthew 12:25; Mark 2:8; Luke 6:8). At times even Jesus' disciples were ashamed to confess what they had been saying, but Jesus knew anyway and confronted them with the truth (Mark 9:30-35). Jesus also knew that not everyone who professed belief in him was trustworthy: "Jesus didn't trust himself to them because he knew all people. He didn't need anyone to tell him about human nature, for he knew what human nature was" (John 2:24-25).

Human nature is prone to make excuses and forget that it's God to whom we must always answer in the end. Jesus and the prophets are here to bring us back to reality.

Arguing With God

Jazz legend Louis Armstrong once declared, "I don't let my mouth say nothin' my head can't stand."[3] Unfortunately the people of Israel had no such scruples. They were saying and doing plenty without checking their heads or hearts to see if it fit with what God wanted.

In his first dispute (Malachi 1:1-5), Malachi points to a part of salvation history that the people of Israel had known all their lives. God honored and blessed Jacob (the people of Israel) instead of Esau (the people of Edom). That blessing and favor continued to this day, but the people denied it. Instead of trusting, they questioned God's faithfulness because God did not do things their way. Malachi foresaw, however, that the people would one day come to their senses and acknowledge the truth that God would work on their behalf beyond the borders of the Promised Land.

The second dispute (1:6–2:9) addresses both priests and people, calling them to task for keeping the best of the land's bounty for themselves and giving God mediocre offerings. Their personal wealth and comfort ranked above the requirements of the covenant, and there was little trust that God would always meet their needs. When wants and needs collide, we usually opt for the wants. Trust and obedience are often further down our to-do list. Astonishingly, Malachi says that the priests found the requirements of Temple sacrifice and worship "tedious" (1:13). They said, "Oh, what a bother!" (1:13).[4] This was their livelihood, their birthright and privilege, yet they groaned about their duties like petulant children.

The Lord of heavenly forces declared that it would be better to shut the Temple doors than to offer polluted, disrespectful sacrifices (see also Leviticus 22:17-25). Such sacrifices are "to no purpose" (1:10)[5] or "in vain" because they do not serve the good purposes of the covenant. Such sacrifices actually did harm by breaking the relationship between God and the people. Because priests and people profaned the altar and the Temple and were insolent, God found "no pleasure" in them (1:10).[6] Instead, other nations acknowledged and feared God as king. It was shameful that God's name was honored "among the nations" (1:11) but not among the chosen people.

A curse would come to anyone who cheated God (1:14), but Malachi announced particularly harsh punishment for priests who disgraced their holy calling (2:1-9). The levitical priesthood (Deuteronomy 18:5) demanded integrity and faithfulness to God's "Instruction" for the welfare of the community. Those who violated this trust faced curses and humiliation.

Malachi's next dispute (Malachi 2:10-16) focuses on the community as a whole, where people were breaking faith with one another and with God. Again, Israel's history as a people led to obvious questions: Aren't we all God's children? Aren't we a family as much as a nation? One manifestation of their unfaithfulness was the worship of foreign gods. "Judah has broken faith; abhorrent things have been done in Israel and in Jerusalem. For Judah has profaned what is holy to the LORD—what He desires—and espoused daughters of alien gods" (2:11).[7] Marrying foreign women was not a problem (Numbers 12:1-9), but worship of their gods was. The punishment for this was expulsion from the community of faith so that they and their descendants did not pollute the true worship of God.

Men in the community were also breaking faith within their own families by divorcing their wives. They "cheated" their wives and their covenant responsibilities. The Hebrew text of verse 15 is not completely certain, but one possible translation is, "Did not the One make [all,] so that all remaining life-breath is His? And what does that One seek but godly folk? So be careful of your life-breath, and let no one break faith with the wife of his youth."[8] The community of faith needed strong families in which children ("godly offspring," 2:15) were brought up to carry God's "spirit" or "life-breath" within themselves and on into the future. The exact meaning of verse 16 is also uncertain but has the sense of flaunting sin like you would show off a new garment. Mixing worship of God with worship of foreign gods did "violence" to the covenant community. This undermined its very reason for existence because it destroyed their relationship with God, their "father" and Creator.

In the fourth dispute (2:17–3:5), God's patience with the people was wearing thin because they questioned God's integrity. Ignoring their own culpability, they accused and even insulted God by claiming God actually "delights" in evildoers (2:17). They demanded that God act with "justice" against others, while not looking at their own sins. Malachi countered with a look into the prophetic future that may have been more than they bargained for. God's messenger is coming to prepare the way for "the LORD whom you are seeking" (3:1). Their satisfaction may have been short-lived, however, because this messenger would come to judge and purify the priests and the people, who sinned against God and one another. Other prophets, too, warned of such a day of judgment (for example, Amos 5:18-20; Zephaniah 1:7-18). Malachi's message is clear that the Lord of heavenly forces comes in power with God's ultimate purposes in mind. We need to be careful about what we ask for and be ready for God's inevitable answer.

Malachi's fifth dispute (Malachi 3:6-12) takes the people to task for their fickleness and backsliding. He gave them hope, however, because God had remained patient and forgiving, allowing "the children of Jacob" to survive and repent yet again. The Hebrew word that is translated "deceive" (Common English Bible) or "defraud" (*The Prophets*) in verse 8 is a pun on the name of Jacob, who was a deceiver and cheater (Genesis 27:34-36). These children of Jacob were following their ancestor's devious ways, which was all plain to God. Malachi delivered a challenge: Put God to the test. Be faithful in your covenant tithes and generous in your trust. Then, says the prophet, the Lord of creation will respond with an out-pouring of bounty and protection. Malachi's challenge is for us, too. We are also Jacob's children and have the freedom to move from struggle and curses to obedience and blessing.

All of this sounds great, but Malachi wasn't finished. The sixth dispute (Malachi 3:13–4:3) again brings the people's charge that God ignores evil. "It is useless to serve God. What have we gained by keeping His charge and walking in abject awe of the LORD of Hosts? And so, we account the arrogant happy: they have indeed done evil and endured; they have indeed dared God and escaped" (3:14-15).[9] And they were not even willing to admit that they were saying such awful things ("What have we spoken about you?" 3:13). How often have we thought or said something similar?

In our limited and flawed view, faithfulness can sometimes seem like a foolish waste of time.

Malachi does not forget those who truly revere God and whose faith-filled words reach God's ears. Their names are recorded in a "scroll of remembrance" (3:16; like the "Lamb's scroll of life," Revelation 21:27) so that they will be spared on the coming Day of Judgment. Then there will be no doubt about who reaps the rewards of righteous living. The dawn of a new day of righteousness will bring healing (literally, "with healing in the corners of its garments"), renewed vigor among the faithful, and victory over wickedness. This dawn fully breaks with Jesus, who does come with healing in the corners of his clothes (Mark 5:24-29; Luke 1:78-79).

Malachi's prophetic disputes reveal a community of faith that was disobedient and immature to the point of blaming God for their own shortcomings. "You don't love us" is the foundational charge they laid against God. We may do the same, or even say, "There is no God," when we don't get our way or we get tired of obedience. Believing that God does not care gives us the green light for pride, selfishness, greed, impurity, insolence, and a host of other offenses against God and other people. Malachi is here to tell us that God does care, God is paying attention, and God is taking names.

A Stern Conclusion

Malachi and the Old Testament draw to a close with a warning and a word of hope (4:4-6). The prophet offers one more reminder about where to turn for "Instruction" in faithful living. He says to look to Moses, the great Lawgiver and the one who saw God face to face (Deuteronomy 34:10-12). In the covenant and instruction that Moses brings, Israel finds its true identity and life as God's people (Deuteronomy 5:1-22).

As further help and as proof of God's continuing care, Elijah is coming to Israel once again. He is identified by some as "the messenger of the covenant" in Malachi 3:1, who precedes God's purifying judgment. In Malachi's conclusion, Elijah comes to reconcile families and heal strife. Unfaithful parents are producing unfaithful children who do not carry God's life-giving spirit (Malachi 2:14-15). They break faith with one another and with God, and they must be made whole before that terrifying day. If not, the people and the land will suffer "utter destruction."[10]

In the New Testament, after Moses and Elijah appear with Jesus in the presence of Peter, James, and John, Jesus says that Elijah has returned to earth in the person of John the Baptist (Mark 9:2-13). Both Malachi and Jesus knew that we need all the help we can get. Malachi had absolute trust in God's goodness toward those who truly love and serve God. He was also absolutely sure that what we say and do makes a profound difference for blessing or for cursing. The choice is ours.

Live the Bible Story

One of Charles Dickens's most memorable characters is Marley's ghost. He is the first of four spirits to visit Ebenezer Scrooge on that fateful Christmas Eve in Dickens's *A Christmas Carol*. Marley is shackled to heavy chains and moneyboxes that represent his obsession in life with accumulating wealth. In death he is doomed to wander for eternity, dragging his chains and wailing with regret that he no longer has the chance to be charitable and generous. He now has a heart for the needs of others but can do nothing about it, except to warn his old partner Ebenezer against continuing to follow the same path.

From Micah all the way through Malachi, it seems that the people of Israel are dragging around the same old chains of unbelief, pride, arrogance, greed, idolatry, and injustice. Yet generation after generation of prophets show that God is willing to send help and to work with God's wayward children. "Return to me," God says, "and I will return to you" (Malachi 3:7).

How do we return? Malachi says that we need proper fear and respect for the Lord of heavenly forces. This all-powerful God is also right at our elbow, which can be both unsettling and comforting. We can trust that nothing escapes God's attention, even though we may think that arrogant evildoers are the smart ones in this world. Malachi shows us that we are free to question God and confidently expect answers, but on God's terms, not ours. God's loving care for God's people is evident every day. We just need to quit feeling sorry for ourselves and acknowledge it. Malachi also says that we should be generous in our tithes and generous in our trust. God has issued the challenge, "Put me to the test." Day after day, we are to offer God our best. In that lies the path of life and blessing.

1. From *http://www.candidcamera.com/cc2/cc2k.html*.
2. From *http://www.tlc.com/tv-shows/what-not-to-wear*.
3. From *Courage to Change: One Day at a Time in Al-Alon II* (Al-Anon Family Group Headquarters, Inc., 1992); page 16.
4. From *The Prophets: The New JPS Translation of the Holy Scriptures According to the Traditional Hebrew Text* (The Jewish Publication Society of America, 1978); page 894.
5. *The Prophets*; page 894.
6. *The Prophets*; page 894.
7. *The Prophets*; page 895.
8. *The Prophets*; page 895.
9. *The Prophets*; page 897.
10. *The Prophets*; page 898.

8.

The Minor Prophets: Information, Inspiration, Blessing, and Change

Micah—Malachi

Claim Your Story

George Washington Carver (1864–1943) is called "the people's scientist" for his dedication to applying scientific discoveries to everyday life. He once wrote, "The primary idea in all of my work was to help the farmer and fill the poor man's empty dinner pail."[1] His groundbreaking work in agriculture and plant science was always focused on improving people's lives by helping them become healthier and more productive.

Carver was born into slavery, orphaned as an infant, and afflicted with frail health as a child. Despite these severe challenges, he nurtured a lifelong passion for the natural world and an abiding curiosity about how it works. He also maintained a deep compassion for others, particularly for the poor. Carver was brilliant, tenacious, and kindhearted and is remembered as a great humanitarian as well as a scientist. His innovations in both basic and applied science laid the groundwork for today's organic farming practices. He also did pioneering research into bio-fuels and numerous plant-based products.

Carver had a deep faith in God, whom he called "the Great Creator." Concerning some of the Creator's gifts in nature, he once said, "I believe the Great Creator has put oils and ores on this earth to give us a breathing spell. As we exhaust them, we must prepare to fall back on our farms...For we can learn to synthesize materials for every human need from the things that grow."[2] He was determined to unlock as many secrets of the Creator's world as he could and then use this knowledge for the benefit of all.

Carver was at ease with his faith and his life as a scientist, finding no conflict between his work and his faith. Instead, he saw a profound harmony in the two. When asked about the relationship between science and divine inspiration, Carver declared, "Inspiration is never at variance with information. In fact, the more information one has, the greater will be the inspiration."[3]

The Minor Prophets would say "Amen" to that. They bring us information about God—what God is like and what God expects of us. They also tell us about God's plans for God's people and for the world. And as far as the prophets are concerned, prophetic information, if it is humbly received, always leads to divine inspiration and blessing. Are we diligent and humble enough to receive what they offer and to be inspired?

Enter the Bible Story

Over a two-hundred-year span, Micah, Nahum, Habakkuk, Zephaniah, Haggai, Zechariah, and Malachi lived through some of the most difficult times that God's people ever faced. They persevered through war, exile, hunger, fear, and fatigue, as well as apathy and outright hostility toward themselves and their messages. They do not offer us theoretical homilies on faithful living but instead show us what it means to truly live for the Lord. The prophets are flesh-and-blood character models: "Brothers and sisters, take the prophets who spoke in the name of the Lord as an example of patient resolve and steadfastness" (James 5:10).

When they tell us to shape up, it's because they knew firsthand how devastating the consequences of sin can be. When they declare that redemption and hope are ours for the asking, they offer us a tried-by-fire hope that can stand up to anything the world sends our way. We can trust them to have our best interest at heart, especially when they sound the toughest: "The prophets, who long ago foretold the grace that you've received, searched and explored, inquiring carefully about this salvation. . . . It was revealed to them that in their search they were not serving themselves but you" (1 Peter 1:10, 12). They speak God's word with zeal and with a never-say-die confidence that their messages are for our immediate good and our ultimate salvation.

God and the Minor Prophets

Across generations the prophets show us many sides of God's character and what God expects from us. They say that God is the Creator of life and the Lord of all. As the one and only God, there is no question that we should respect and obey him. Yet this awe-inspiring and all-powerful God knows us, loves us, and is with us every day. It is our privilege and responsibility to know, love, and live close to God.

God is just, righteous, loving, forgiving, and trustworthy. We are to be exactly the same toward God and one another. The prophets' own ministries testify to the fact that God does not leave us in the dark about what God expects from us. To the contrary, God speaks to us through the Spirit, the covenant, and the prophets, as well as through human history and the natural world. Godly wisdom is available for anyone who truly seeks it. No matter how dark the times, the prophets reassure us that God's plans for us and for the world are trustworthy and good. We are asked to accept that both judgment and redemption are part of these plans. Each will be accomplished in God's time and in God's way.

Minor Prophets in the New Testament

When we turn from the Old Testament to the New, we find the Minor Prophets again. They are a major presence from Matthew through Revelation. Sometimes they are quoted directly, and other times specific prophecies are echoed by New Testament writers. Jesus, John, Paul, and others took up the great prophetic themes of justice and righteousness and of punishment and redemption. And Jesus declared unequivocally that he was the promised one whom the prophets longed to see (Matthew 13:16-17). Jesus, John, and others in the New Testament also drew heavily on prophecies about the Day of the Lord, which brings judgment to sinners and salvation to the righteous.

The New Testament writers know Jesus as Emmanuel, the long-awaited Messiah. They show us how Jesus fulfills the prophets' hopes for the Messiah, the one who comes to deliver God's people.

Birth, Ministry, and Passion of Jesus

- Micah 5:2. Jesus is born in Bethlehem. Matthew 2:5-6; John 7:41-42.
- Micah 5:4-5. Jesus is a great king in the line of David and a shepherd of his people. Luke 1:32.
- Micah 7:20. God's promises to Abraham's descendants are fulfilled in Jesus. Luke 1:54-55.
- Zephaniah 3:15. Jesus is the promised king of Israel. John 1:49.
- Malachi 3:2. Jesus judges and refines his people. Matthew 3:10-12.
- Malachi 3:6. God and Christ do not change in their love toward us. Hebrews 13:8; James 1:17-18.
- Malachi 4:2. Jesus is a light from God to bring wisdom and peace. Luke 1:78-79; 1 John 1:5-7.
- Micah 5:1. Jesus suffers abuse for his people. Matthew 26:67; John 18:22.
- Zechariah 11:12-13. Thirty pieces of silver are traitorous "wages." Matthew 26:14-15; 27:3-10.
- Zechariah 12:10. Jesus is "pierced" for the people's sin. John 19:36-37.
- Zechariah 13:7. Jesus the Shepherd Messiah is struck and his flock scattered. Matthew 26:31; Mark 14:27.

Teaching of Jesus

- Micah 6:6-8. We are to show justice and mercy toward others, humility and love toward God. Matthew 7:12; Mark 12:33.
- Haggai 2:12. It is God and God's altar that are holy and that make our gifts holy. Matthew 23:19.
- Zechariah 9:9. Jesus is a humble and gentle king. Matthew 11:29; 21:2-5; John 12:14-15.

- Zechariah 9:11. Jesus' blood of the covenant gives release and pardon. Matthew 26:27-28.
- Zechariah 11:15-17. In stark contrast to the uncaring shepherd who forsakes the flock, Jesus comes as the Good Shepherd who lays down his life for his sheep. John 10:1, 8-13.
- Zechariah 13:1. Jesus offers the cleansing and saving water of life. John 4:10-14; Revelation 21:6.
- Zechariah 14:21. Jesus drives merchants from God's house. John 2:15-16.
- Malachi 2:8-9. Jesus denounces corrupt leaders who burden God's people. Matthew 23:1-36.
- Malachi 3:1. John the Baptist is God's messenger, who comes to prepare the way for Jesus. Matthew 11:7-10; Mark 1:1-3; Luke 7:24-28.
- Malachi 4:5-6. John is Elijah, who returns before the Messiah appears. Matthew 11:13-15; 17:10-13; Luke 1:17.

Day of Judgment and Salvation

- Micah 7:6. Family members will turn against one another. Matthew 10:21, 35-36.
- Habakkuk 2:3-4. To please God, we must endure in faith until the end. Hebrews 10:37-38; Romans 1:17; Galatians 3:11.
- Zechariah 14:7. Judgment Day is known only to God and brings a new kind of light from God. Matthew 24:36; Acts 1:6-7; Revelation 22:5.
- Malachi 3:5. Oppression and injustice will be punished. 2 Thessalonians 2:12; James 5:4.
- Malachi 3:16. God's faithful servants will be remembered and saved. Revelation 20:12; 21:27.

About the Christian Faith

The Prophets Go Baroque

If you sing in a choir, whether church, civic, or professional, odds are that you have sung George Frideric Handel's *Messiah*. Haggai, Malachi, and Zechariah are an integral part of Handel's great oratorio, which is one of the most beloved and most performed sacred works in the history of music. *Messiah* was first performed at a benefit concert in Dublin, Ireland, in April 1742. So eager were people to hear Handel's new work that the concert hall management asked ladies to wear dresses with no hoops so that more people could get into the hall.[4] After thousands of performances, concertgoers are still eager to hear *Messiah,* which presents a history of salvation using Scriptures from the King James Version of the Bible. Part one of the oratorio is based on prophecies about the coming Messiah and the fulfillment of these prophecies in Jesus Christ. With texts from Haggai 2:6-7 and Malachi 3:1-2, a bass soloist proclaims, "Thus Saith the Lord," and then asks, "But Who May Abide the Day of His Coming?" The chorus responds with "And He Shall Purify," based on Malachi 3:3. After the birth of Jesus is announced, a soprano soloist calls God's people to "Rejoice Greatly, O Daughter of Zion," from Zechariah 9:9-10.

Handel celebrates God's great gift of Christ. Each time *Messiah* is sung, Haggai, Zechariah, and Malachi are front and center, asking us once again to watch, listen, and rejoice at God's saving grace.

Though this is not an exhaustive list, it is impressive to see just how influential the Minor Prophets are in the New Testament, especially Micah, Zechariah, and Malachi. However, their influence extends even further. The apostle Paul was a self-described "Hebrew of the Hebrews" and a Pharisee (Philippians 3:5) who knew his Bible and the Prophets well. He said, "Whatever was written in the past was written for our instruction so that we could have hope through endurance and through the encouragement of the scriptures" (Romans 15:4). Paul found great encouragement and inspiration in the Minor Prophets, and he passes this on to us.

Teaching of Paul

• Nahum 1:15. God sends messengers of peace and good news. Romans 10:15.

- Zechariah 8:16. We must always speak the truth to one another. Ephesians 4:25.
- Zechariah 9:10. Christ is our peace and brings reconciliation with God to all people. Ephesians 2:14-18.
- Malachi 1:2-3. It is God's choice to show love, mercy, and compassion or to withhold it. Romans 9:13-15.
- Malachi 2:10. For believers there is one God, one faith, and one Lord. 1 Corinthians 8:6; Ephesians 4:5-6.
- Malachi 3:10. God is generous with God's blessings if we are generous in our trust. 2 Corinthians 9:6-8.

When Paul preached in the synagogue in Antioch (Acts 13:38-41), he quoted Habakkuk 1:5 as a warning to anyone who would scoff at God's promises or not believe that God is at work among God's people. Along with the warning, Paul also gave a promise: "Through Jesus everyone who believes is put in right relationship with God" (Acts 13:39). Having a right relationship with God is of utmost concern for the prophets, too. It's what they strove for themselves, and it's how they want us to live. As we understand their impact on the New Testament, we see how they are part of the stream of knowledge and divine inspiration that begins in the Old Testament and flows on into the New, culminating in the "living water" that Jesus offers.

Information, Inspiration, and Change

The prophets tell us the truth, and they point us to Jesus. They aim to set us on the right path in life and to bring us back when we wander. In the light of God's truth, they know we can mend our broken ways and change for the better. They don't let up or make excuses for us. They just speak the truth and fully expect us to make the most of it.

It wasn't an easy road for them. Micah cried out in grief like a jackal, and Habakkuk believed that God was ignoring his heartrending pleas for help. We can be fearful or feel overwhelmed or just do something sinful despite our best intentions. Paul speaks for all of us when he says, "I don't do the good that I want to do, but I do the evil that I don't want to do. . . . I'm a miserable human being" (Romans 7:19, 24). As miserable as we may be, we know that's not the whole story. God breaks into our misery and sin to send us new words of revelation and new calls to repentance and hope.

Three people in the New Testament are stellar examples of hopeful change. Each heard God's word through Jesus, the Word made flesh. Each took the Word to heart and grew more fully into the person God created them to be.

Paul, who was also known as Saul, was an ardent defender of the Jewish faith and a persecutor of Christians (Philippians 3:5-6). All this changed when Jesus confronted him on the road to Damascus. "Who are you, Lord?" Paul asked. "I am Jesus, whom you are harassing," was the reply (Acts 9:5). Paul had three days of blindness in which to decide whether or not he was going to take this revelation to heart. Paul did take Jesus' words to heart and did change. Paul went on to be a great missionary for Christ and to write about one fourth of the New Testament. Forever after, to everyone who will listen, he declares, "[Jesus] is God's Son" (Acts 9:20).

As a disciple, Peter was strong, hot tempered, and insightful. He could also be amazingly off the mark. One minute he declared that Jesus was "the Christ, the Son of the living God" (Matthew 16:16). Then, he forcefully rejected the truth that Jesus tried to teach him, to the point that Jesus called him "Satan" and said Peter was "not thinking God's thoughts but human thoughts" (verse 23). The night before the Crucifixion, Peter even denied knowing Jesus (John 18:15-27). Yet Peter repented and matured in his faith. He went on to be one of the founding fathers of the church (Acts 2).

Martha of Bethany, along with her sister Mary and brother Lazarus, was a friend of Jesus. On one of his visits in their home, Jesus chided Martha for being too busy with practical matters to truly listen to what he was saying. She could not hear "the better part" because she was distracted and annoyed (Luke 10:41-42). Yet, when we see Martha again, she is a changed woman. On one of the worst days of her life, when her beloved brother lay dead in his tomb, Jesus said to her, "I am the resurrection and the life. . . . Do you believe this?" With no hesitation she replied, "Yes, Lord, I believe that you are the Christ, God's Son, the one who is coming into the world" (John 11:25-27). Martha's response to Jesus shows that she was willing to slow down and to listen. Through her willingness to change, she found that Jesus was her Lord and Savior as well as her friend.

God did not give up on Paul, Peter, or Martha, and God does not give up on us. We just need ears to truly hear, a willing spirit, and a heart for God's Word.

As we learn and grow with the Word, we become part of God's great legacy of revelation. We stand in the lineage of the prophets, receiving the Word through them but also being called to make it our own. The Holy Spirit is always at hand to add fresh insight to the knowledge we gain. As Haggai 2:5 tells us, "[God's] spirit stands in your midst. / Don't fear." One of the beauties of Scripture is that it continually gives us new knowledge of God and God's ways. The prophets spoke to their unique times and circumstances, and they also speak to ours. They offer specific truths that are timeless in their applications. God's Word always has something to say about where we are and where we need to be. God knows all about our current mess and how to help us out of it. The prophets offer unequivocal assurance that God knows us, understands us, loves us, and wants us back when we stray. God's Word can always reach us and offer us hope.

Live the Story

"Nothing is begun and perfected at the same time." So says Miles Smith in his preface to the first edition of the King James Version of the Bible, which was published in 1611.[5] This applies to our lives just as it does to the art and science of biblical translation. We begin with God and keep working toward perfection. When we need help, the prophets are always there to remind, to strengthen, and to inspire us:

> He has told you, human one,
> what is good and
> what the LORD requires from you:

to do justice, embrace faithful love,
and walk humbly with your God.
(Micah 6:8)

The LORD is good,
a haven in a day of distress.
He acknowledges those
who take refuge in him. (Nahum 1:7)

I will rejoice in the LORD.
I will rejoice in the God
of my deliverance.
The LORD God is my strength.
(Habakkuk 3:18-19)

The LORD your God is in your midst—
a warrior bringing victory.
He will create calm with his love;
he will rejoice over you with singing.
(Zephaniah 3:17)

Be strong, all you people
of the land, says the LORD.
Work, for I am with you. . . .
My spirit stands in your midst.
Don't fear. (Haggai 2:4-5)

They will be my people, and I will be
their God—in truth and in righteousness. (Zechariah 8:8)

Return to me and I will return to you,
says the LORD of heavenly forces.
(Malachi 3:7)

The prophets always offer hope, even though they harbor no illusions about us. Our strengths and weaknesses are plain to them and to God. Prophets know firsthand the terrible consequences of our failures. They also know that God's unfailing love will never let us go.

In the process of learning the difference between grownups and children, a little three-year-old girl once called adults "growing ups." This is an apt description of believers. We should all be "growing ups" in knowledge, inspiration, and faith. The prophets expect no less of us and have every confidence that we can do it. We can rely on them and on God to be with us every step of the way. Like Paul, we can be absolutely sure that "the one who started a good work in you will stay with you to complete the job by the day of Christ Jesus" (Philippians 1:6).

1. From *http://archive.fieldmuseum.org/carver/pdf/Carver_Guide.pdf*.
2. From *http://fieldmuseum.org/about/george-washington-carver-main-press-release*.
3. From *George Washington Carver: A Biography*, by Gary R. Kremer (Greenwood Publishing Group, 2011); page 116.
4. From *http://www.smithsonianmag.com/arts-culture/The-Glorious-History-of-Handels-Messiah.html*.
5. From *In the Beginning*, by Alister McGrath (Anchor Books, 2001); page192.

Leader Guide

People often view the Bible as a maze of obscure people, places, and events from centuries ago and struggle to relate it to their daily lives. IMMERSION invites us to experience the Bible as a record of God's loving revelation to humankind. These studies recognize our emotional, spiritual, and intellectual needs and welcome us into the Bible story and into deeper faith.

As leader of an IMMERSION group, you will help participants to encounter the Word of God and the God of the Word that will lead to new creation in Christ. You do not have to be an expert to lead; in fact, you will participate with your group in listening to and applying God's life-transforming Word to your lives. You and your group will explore the building blocks of the Christian faith through key stories, people, ideas, and teachings in every book of the Bible. You will also explore the bridges and points of connection between the Old and New Testaments.

Choosing and Using the Bible

The central goal of IMMERSION is engaging the members of your group with the Bible in a way that informs their minds, forms their hearts, and transforms the way they live out their Christian faith. Participants will need this study book and a Bible. IMMERSION is an excellent accompaniment to the Common English Bible (CEB). It shares with the CEB four common aims: clarity of language, faith in the Bible's power to transform lives, the emotional expectation that people will find the love of God, and the rational expectation that people will find the knowledge of God.

Other recommended study Bibles include *The New Interpreter's Study Bible* (NRSV), *The New Oxford Annotated Study Bible* (NRSV), *The HarperCollins Study Bible* (NRSV), the *NIV and TNIV Study Bibles*, and the *Archaeological Study Bible* (NIV). Encourage participants to use more than one translation. *The Message: The Bible in Contemporary Language* is a modern paraphrase of the Bible, based on the original languages. Eugene H. Peterson has created a masterful presentation of the Scripture text, which is best used alongside rather than in place of the CEB or another primary English translation.

One of the most reliable interpreters of the Bible's meaning is the Bible itself. Invite participants first of all to allow Scripture to have its say. Pay attention to context. Ask questions of the text. Read every passage with curiosity, always seeking to answer the basic Who? What? Where? When? and Why? questions.

Bible study groups should also have handy essential reference resources in case someone wants more information or needs clarification on specific words, terms, concepts, places, or people mentioned in the Bible. A Bible dictionary, Bible atlas, concordance, and one-volume Bible commentary together make for a good, basic reference library.

The Leader's Role

An effective leader prepares ahead. This leader guide provides easy-to-follow, step-by-step suggestions for leading a group. The key task of the leader is to guide discussion and activities that will engage heart and head and will invite faith development. Discussion questions are included, and you may want to add questions posed by you or your group. Here are suggestions for helping your group engage Scripture:

State questions clearly and simply.

Ask questions that move Bible truths from "outside" (dealing with concepts, ideas, or information about a passage) to "inside" (relating to the experiences, hopes, and dreams of the participants).

Work for variety in your questions, including compare and contrast, information recall, motivation, connections, speculation, and evaluation.

Avoid questions that call for yes-or-no responses or answers that are obvious.

Don't be afraid of silence during a discussion. It often yields especially thoughtful comments.

Test questions before using them by attempting to answer them yourself.

When leading a discussion, pay attention to the mood of your group by "listening" with your eyes as well as your ears.

Guidelines for the Group

IMMERSION is designed to promote full engagement with the Bible for the purpose of growing faith and building up Christian community. While much can be gained from individual reading, a group Bible study offers an ideal setting in which to achieve these aims. Encourage participants to bring their Bibles and read from Scripture during the session. Invite participants to consider the following guidelines as they participate in the group:

Respect differences of interpretation and understanding.

Support one another with Christian kindness, compassion, and courtesy.

Listen to others with the goal of understanding rather than agreeing or disagreeing.

Celebrate the opportunity to grow in faith through Bible study.

Approach the Bible as a dialogue partner, open to the possibility of being challenged or changed by God's Word.

Recognize that each person brings unique and valuable life experiences to the group and is an important part of the community.

Reflect theologically—that is, be attentive to three basic questions: What does this say about God? What does this say about me/us? What does this say about the relationship between God and me/us?

Commit to a lived faith response in light of insights you gain from the Bible. In other words, what changes in attitudes (how you believe) or actions (how you behave) are called for by God's Word?

Group Sessions

The group sessions, like the chapters themselves, are built around three sections: "Claim Your Story," "Enter the Bible Story," and "Live the Story." Sessions are designed to move participants from an awareness of their own life story, issues, needs, and experiences into an encounter and dialogue with the story of Scripture and to make decisions integrating their personal stories and the Bible's story.

The session plans in the following pages will provide questions and activities to help your group focus on the particular content of each chapter. In addition to questions and activities, the plans will include chapter title, Scripture, and faith focus.

Here are things to keep in mind for all the sessions:

Prepare Ahead

Study the Scripture, comparing different translations and perhaps a paraphrase.

Read the chapter, and consider what it says about your life and the Scripture.

Gather materials such as large sheets of paper or a markerboard with markers.

Prepare the learning area. Write the faith focus for all to see.

Welcome Participants

Invite participants to greet one another.

Tell them to find one or two people and talk about the faith focus.

Ask: What words stand out for you? Why?

Guide the Session

Look together at "Claim Your Story." Ask participants to give their reactions to the stories and examples given in each chapter. Use questions from the session plan to elicit comments based on personal experiences and insights.

Ask participants to open their Bibles and "Enter the Bible Story." For each portion of Scripture, use questions from the session plan to help participants gain insight into the text and relate it to issues in their own lives.

Step through the activity or questions posed in "Live the Story." Encourage participants to embrace what they have learned and to apply it in their daily lives.

Invite participants to offer their responses or insights about the boxed material in "Across the Testaments," "About the Scripture," and "About the Christian Faith."

Close the Session

Encourage participants to read the following week's Scripture and chapter before the next session.

Offer a closing prayer.

1. The Minor Prophets: Noise, Light, and Hope
Micah—Malachi

Faith Focus

God calls ordinary people to extraordinary tasks. Our part is to be available. God supplies the wisdom and the strength.

Before the Session

Gather a compass, a GPS, a map, printed driving directions from your home to another location, a recipe, an instruction manual for assembling a bookshelf or similar household item, and other sources of directions and instructions. Before your group arrives, arrange these on a table or other prominent place. Also make sure you have a copy of the Bible on hand.

If possible, obtain a penlight or other small, portable flashlight for every person in your group. You can find these at discount, drug, home improvement, and office supply stores.

Claim Your Story

Call attention to the items you have displayed and ask the group to suggest what they have in common. How are they alike? How are they different? When do we use them? How do they make our lives easier?

Connect these items to the role of Scripture in our lives. Offer a personal example of how the Bible has provided direction for you as you have faced uncertainty and decisions. Then encourage others in the group to do the same. Acknowledge that many Christians avoid or ignore the Minor Prophets because of their forceful, blunt, and controversial messages and because they seem so far removed from our lives and circumstances. Affirm that their messages can help us better understand who God is, what God is like, and what God expects of us. Stress that in spite of their dire warnings about the consequences of disobedience, the Minor Prophets remind us that regardless of how terrible things are or how uncertain we may be, there is always hope.

Enter the Bible Story

Ask the group to define or explain what a prophet is. Using information in "Called for Hard Times," lead them to compare and contrast their ideas with the writer's description of biblical prophets. List the twelve Minor Prophets on a board or chart, and circle the seven that comprise this study. Then briefly describe the circumstances of God's people during the ministries of the prophets, and relate what we know about them as individuals.

To help the group begin thinking about the messages of the prophets, ask volunteers to describe the hardest thing they have ever had to say to someone. What were the circumstances? What was the message? How was it received? What were the results? Be prepared to offer a personal example to encourage others to respond.

Using the information in "Called to Speak," review the qualities and characteristics of the prophetic word. Cite examples from this section that illustrate its different functions. Then explain prophetic messages in the form of visions and sign acts. Ask a volunteer to read aloud Micah 3:9-12 to illustrate an announcement of judgment; then ask someone to read aloud Nahum 1:12-13 as an example of an announcement of hope.

Lead the group to explore the idea that the biblical prophets were called to reconcile God's people to their destiny. Ask: What was this destiny? What had put it in jeopardy? What was their essential message to God's people in this regard?

Summarize for the group the teaching role of the prophets. Stress the fact that while they did not hesitate to call attention to sin and disobedience, their final word is one of hope and confidence in God's ultimate goal of salvation and redemption for us.

Live the Story

Recall the story attributed to Abraham Lincoln about the traveler in the thunderstorm. Read aloud the man's petition: "Oh Lord! If it's all the same to you, give us a little more light and a little less noise!"

Remind the group about the "noisy" times in which the Minor Prophets lived and ministered. Then ask: Where is there "noise" in our world? in your life? How does this noise prevent you from hearing the voice of God? How does it threaten your faith?

Give everyone a penlight or small flashlight; then dim or extinguish the lights in the room. Ask group members, one or a few at a time, to turn on their lights as you make the following supplications:

- Grant us spiritual ears to hear your voice amid the noise of the world and of our lives.
- Teach us more of who you are and what your expectations are for us.
- Confront us with our sin and disobedience, and extend to us your forgiveness and mercy.
- Give us the courage to be faithful to your way and your call in our lives, even when it is difficult to discern and follow.
- Shed light on the paths of our lives. Give us both light to see our own way and light to share with others.
- Speak to us your message of hope and reconciliation, and help us in turn to share this message with those around us.

Close by saying, "Lord, hear our prayer."

2. Micah: A Regular Guy "Who Is Like the Lord"
Micah

Faith Focus

For our own good, God requires us to do right by others, to love what God loves, and to live like we know that God is in charge.

Before the Session

Prepare index cards with the group assignments from "Enter the Bible Story" below.

Claim Your Story

Begin by describing to the group a time in your life when you had the opportunity to choose between doing a very difficult thing and taking the easy way out. What were the circumstances? What did you decide, and why? What were the results?

Invite others in the group to share similar experiences. Then recall for the group the example of Sir Robert Shirley and Staunton Harold Church. Read aloud the inscription that appears above the door of Shirley's church, which he did not live to see completed. Note that like Shirley, the prophet Micah chose the more difficult way, the better way, God's way, rather than taking the easy way out. Remind the group that the inscription at Shirley's church quotes part of Psalm 112:6 (KJV): "The righteous shall be in everlasting remembrance," affirming that God sees and remembers our faithfulness.

Enter the Bible Story

Using the information in "Micah's Times," provide the limited background information about Micah that we know. Then describe the circumstances of Judah and Israel and why God's people needed a prophet. Ask: Why do you think God called Micah for this task? Why do you think Micah agreed to do it? What was at stake for God's people if they did not turn from the prevailing corruption, injustice, and tolerance of pagan worship?

Offer a brief review of the way Micah presented his messages, using the information in "Micah's Messages." Call attention to Micah's verbal skills by reading the examples provided from the Moffatt translation of Scripture. Affirm that while Micah proclaimed God's judgment against the people and the punishment they would endure, he resolutely held to his faith and trust in God.

Divide into two small groups and make the following assignments:

Group 1: Review "Micah's Messages of Judgment" and make a list of the "charges" against God's people. Who was guilty, and what were they guilty of? Select some key verses from the Bible to illustrate the charges.

Group 2: Review "Micah's Messages of Hope" and make a list of the things Micah says will eventually happen. What could God's people look forward to? Select some key verses from the Bible to illustrate the good things the people would experience in the future.

Recall for the group the conversation of the couple in the comic strip. Lead the group to summarize what Micah says about how we are to live and learn. Ask a volunteer to read aloud Micah 6:8; ask others to read aloud Matthew 7:12 and Mark 12:29-31. Ask group members to suggest what they think it means for us to "walk humbly with God." Then ask: According to Micah, what does God love? How do we show we love what God loves? How do we live like we know that God is in charge?

Live the Story

Recall for the group the psychotherapist's voice mail greeting and connect it, as the writer has done, to what Micah challenges us to do. Ask them to close their eyes and silently consider their responses to these questions:

- Who are you in relation to God?
- How does your relationship with God affect your relationships with others?
- When have you tried to live life apart from God? What were the results? What drew you back to God?
- When has God given you hope for a fresh start?
- Are you so committed to wanting God above all else that you strive to do "the best things in the worst times and hope for God's best in the most calamitous"?

Close with a prayer for courage to say "yes" to God even in the worst of times, to live securely in who you are as God's people, and "to do justice, embrace faithful love, and walk humbly with your God."

3. Nahum, Habakkuk, and Zephaniah: The Perils of Power and Pride
Nahum, Habakkuk, and Zephaniah

Faith Focus

The prophets provide a straightforward look at what happens when we make bad choices in life and at the "pay day" that is sure to follow. They also are confident of a better outcome when we make good, faithful choices.

Before the Session

Ahead of time, search online for quotes and pithy sayings about power, pride, and control. Select a dozen or so, and print these on individual sheets of paper to make mini-posters. Include those from Proverbs and C. S. Lewis that the writer mentions. Attach the posters to the walls of your meeting area.

Prepare the small group assignments as described in "Enter the Bible Story."

Claim Your Story

Call attention to the various quotations about power and pride, and ask volunteers to select some to read aloud. Suggest that the problems of power, pride, and control are as old as humankind. The woman and the man in the garden of Eden ate fruit from the forbidden tree after the snake tempted the woman and told her eating the fruit would make her "like God" (Genesis 3:5). Later, "all people on the earth" wanted to build for themselves "a city and a tower with its top in the sky, and … make a name for" themselves (Genesis 11:1, 4). In both cases, instead of their choices bringing the desired results, the people's relationship with God was broken and they suffered terrible, life-altering, and widespread consequences.

Remind the group of the political, military, and economic circumstances during the time of Nahum, Habakkuk, and Zephaniah. Stress that these prophets confronted power, pride, and the desire to control by reminding God's people that regardless of the circumstances, God, not they and not their political enemies, was in control.

Enter the Bible Story
Using the information in "Challenging Messages for Challenging Times" and "Lord, How Long?" offer a brief overview of Nahum, Habakkuk, and Zephaniah. Acknowledge that the writings of these prophets can be startling. They use graphic imagery and describe unpleasant circumstances that make us wince. Talk briefly about the suffering of the innocent, God's demonstrations of anger in dealing with sin, and the seeming silence of God in the face of the suffering that these prophets describe. Read aloud some of the prophets' laments, such as Habakkuk 1:2, 13, and ask: What can we learn from the prophets here? What do their accounts challenge us to do?

Remind the group that in spite of their vivid descriptions of horrible circumstances, the prophets never stop there. They always provide messages of hope and point to God's goals of redemption, restoration, and justice. They always assure God's people of God's mercy, love, and attentiveness to our cries for help.

Divide the group into three smaller groups and give each group one of the following assignments, printed on an index card or half-sheet of paper:

Group One: Using the information in "Nahum" in Chapter 3 and your Bibles, work together to prepare the following summary: Nahum's focus and basic message; Nahum's description of God; Nahum's prophecies for Nineveh; Nahum's promise for the future.

Group Two: Using the information in "Habakkuk" in Chapter 3 and your Bibles, work together to prepare the following summary: Habakkuk's complaints to and conversation with God; God's response to Habakkuk; God's reasons for sending punishment on Judah; Habakkuk's promise for the future.

Group Three: Using the information in "Zephaniah" in Chapter 3 and your Bibles, work together to prepare the following summary: Zephaniah's pronouncements of judgment; specific individuals Zephaniah condemned and why; what Zephaniah means by "the day of the LORD"; Zephaniah's promise for another "day of the LORD" on the other side of judgment.

Allow the groups adequate time to examine Scripture and prepare their summary statements. Then reassemble the groups and ask each group to present its summary.

Live the Story
Read aloud the Jewish proverb, "God waits long, but he pays with interest." Ask volunteers to explain what they think this means, especially in light of your review of Nahum, Habakkuk, and Zephaniah. Also ask volunteers to distinguish

between the two "pay days" the prophets talk about. Make sure everyone understands the difference between the two.

Close by reading aloud the following prayer, pausing briefly after each paragraph:

> Faithful and merciful God, we confess that we can be prideful and power-hungry. We want to be in control. We sometimes act as though we can do your job. For this, we ask your forgiveness. We're grateful for the messages of the prophets that remind us that you and you alone are God, and you are in control.
>
> We have made poor choices, God. We have made things worse for ourselves and others by our willful acts of disobedience. Forgive us, God, and redeem our lives and our circumstances.
>
> We also confess that we grow weary and impatient as we wait for "the pay day of redemption." We lose faith and question whether you hear us and why you will not respond. As we wait, teach us what we need to learn so that we can live more fully and faithfully as your people.
>
> In the areas of our lives where we have certain power and control, we place these at your disposal and ask you to give us wisdom to use them with humility.
>
> Challenge our priorities, God. Show us where we are wrongly devoted to things other than you. Help us to see all of life and eternity through your eyes, and help us live confidently with the hope that only you can give. Amen.

4. Nahum, Habakkuk, and Zephaniah: Hope for Castoffs
Nahum, Habakkuk, and Zephaniah

Faith Focus
In the face of tragedy, grief, and fear, people of faith put their whole trust in God's goodness and mercy.

Before the Session
On a large piece of posterboard, write "Hope for Castoffs." Attach it to a focal wall in your meeting area. Surround it with several pieces of construction paper. Obtain several pairs of scissors; glue sticks or tape; and a variety of magazines, newspapers, and other printed resources that can be cut apart.

If you have the equipment necessary to display them, locate online images of the Reverend Howard Finster's artwork and select a few to display to your group. Find out more about the artwork ahead of time, including the cast-off items he used to create it and the message he hoped the art would communicate.

Also obtain a recording from a blues musician that speaks of loneliness, doubt, and despair, and the equipment necessary to play the recording. The writer mentions a particular B. B. King song; you may find that one or another one that is suitable.

Claim Your Story
Briefly recall the story of the Reverend Howard Finster. Emphasize that Finster had devoted his life to preaching the gospel for forty-five years before he began painting sacred art. Although his method of proclamation changed, his message did not. He believed that in spite of the bitterness and ugliness we often find in the world, God's purposes are much higher and better. God's purposes are beautiful. Lead the group to evaluate Finster's philosophy and respond to it by asking questions such as these: Do you find it difficult to agree with Finster's philosophy sometimes? Why, or why not? Where do you see evidence of ugliness and bitterness in the world? How does this affect people and how they treat one another? How does this affect people's ability to experience joy and hope?

Spend some time identifying actual events and circumstances—global, national, local, and personal—that have produced hate, bitterness, and ugliness and have squashed people's hope. Be prepared to cite personal examples and encourage others in your group to do the same.

Acknowledge that the biblical prophets do not gloss over sin and its consequences. They warn about and describe in often horrific detail the terrible things that will happen when people fail to honor and respect God and lapse into moral and ethical failure. But judgment is not the whole story, and it's not the end of the story. The biblical prophets offer words of hope, both for those who first heard their messages, and for us.

Distribute scissors and the printed resources you brought. Ask group members to look through them to find headlines, phrases, words, and images that remind them that there is hope, and that the world is still a beautiful place. Ask them to attach these to the construction paper you have placed around the "Hope for Castoffs" poster on the wall.

Enter the Bible Story
Using the information from "Nahum" (pages 40–42), recall for the group the circumstances in which God's people lived at the time of Nahum's prophecy. Briefly explain Assyria's role in this (see Micah 1 as necessary). Then note that Nahum declared that the time had come for Assyria's oppression of God's people to end. They would be punished, and God's people would once again worship God alone and fulfill their covenant promises. Ask volunteers to read aloud the following verses from Nahum to illustrate the hope that he instilled in his messages: 1:3, 7, 12-13, 15; 2:2.

In spite of generations of warnings from prophets about betraying God's trust, God's people did not seem to be listening, and they were suffering the consequences. Remind the group about Habakkuk and the way he questioned and argued with God. He was angry, frustrated, afraid, and tired. He was also unashamedly honest with God. In his discouragement, he received reassurance, and he was able to offer words of hope to God's people. Ask volunteers to read aloud some of the hope-filled messages we find in Habakkuk: 2:14, 20; 3:1-19. Stress that nothing could destroy Habakkuk's faith. He knew that God would redeem God's people. Read aloud the last paragraph of "Habakkuk" on page 43.

Next, acknowledge that what we most likely notice about the prophet Zephaniah are the noise, drama, and fury of the judgment and punishment he declares. Yet Zephaniah offers a great deal of hope as well. Ask volunteers to read aloud some examples, such as Zephaniah 2:7 and 3:9-20. Zephaniah assured God's people that God had great plans for those who sought God and practiced justice, righteousness, and humility. He promised that the faithful remnant, though they might not look like much to anyone else, had great potential as God's community of faith. Read aloud Howard Finster's poem from page 44 and connect what he did through his art to what God can do with "castoffs." If available, display the images of Finster's artwork you found online, and briefly describe what they are made of and the message the artist wanted to convey.

Next, stress Zephaniah's challenge to "seek the LORD." Read aloud Zephaniah 1:6, 2:3, 3:12. Pose the writer's questions: Do we run after God? Do we require God's presence as if our very lives depend upon it?

Suggest that while the prophets saw and heard things that the average person does not, they still offer some very practical advice. Ask the group to help you formulate a list of basic guidelines from the prophets. Ask them to spend a few minutes scanning the short books of Nahum, Habakkuk, and Zephaniah and call out brief statements in their own words that summarize the prophets' messages about how God's people are to live. (The section "Prophetic Back to Basics," pages 45–46, offers some examples. Challenge your group to come up with others as well.) Write the statements on the board.

Live the Story

Play the blues recording you selected. Then ask: Do you think Nahum, Habakkuk, and Zephaniah ever sang the blues? Do you think they ever felt like giving up? What about you? Do you sometimes question whether God is active in the world, or whether God will take care of your needs? When no relief is in sight, how do you hang onto your faith? How do you live faithfully in bitter times?

Challenge the group to claim the prophets' promise that those who genuinely and passionately seek God will not be disappointed. God will respond, and God will redeem. Our hope is in God, and God is working for our good.

Ask the group to close their eyes and offer silent responses as you guide their thoughts in prayer:

- Confess a circumstance or an area of your life that threatens to leave you bitter, angry, resentful, or cold. Ask God to replace this feeling with the sweet spirit of God's presence and a positive, hopeful disposition that reflects God's love and presence in your life.
- Thank God for the beauty of the world and for God's goodness and mercy that overcome the harsh and ugly realities of the world.
- Ask God to show you how best to honor and worship him with gratitude for renewing your life and using you to help achieve divine purposes.

5. Haggai and Zechariah:
Confronting Situational Blindness
Haggai and Zechariah

Faith Focus
God's people are defined not by political or military power nor by prosperity or by poverty. God's children are known by proper worship and covenant living.

Before the Session
Copy on individual index cards the following quotations attributed to Helen Keller:

"I can see, and that is why I can be happy, in what you call the dark, but which to me is golden. I can see a God-made world, not a manmade world."

"Character cannot be developed in ease and quiet. Only through experience of trial and suffering can the soul be strengthened, ambition inspired, and success achieved."

"Unless we form the habit of going to the Bible in bright moments as well as in trouble, we cannot fully respond to its consolations because we lack equilibrium between light and darkness."

"People do not like to think. If one thinks, one must reach conclusions. Conclusions are not always pleasant."

"Faith is the strength by which a shattered world shall emerge into the light."

"The only thing worse than being blind is having sight but no vision."[1]

Claim Your Story
Briefly remind group members about Helen Keller, who became blind and deaf from an illness when she was nineteen months old but went on to become a well-educated and prolific author, speaker, and activist. Distribute the quotations attributed to her among group members and ask them to read these aloud. Pause between each and encourage group members to respond by adding their insights and comments. Connect some of her thoughts to the circumstances in which God's people lived at the time of Haggai and Zechariah: they had experienced trials and suffering; they had lived 'in the dark'; they had at times become hopeless and thought they had no future; through the prophets, they had been forced to look honestly at themselves, and what they saw was not pleasant; they had been challenged by the prophets to hold onto their faith and continue to worship and live in covenant relationship with God.

Suggest that the prophets Haggai and Zechariah confronted God's people at a time of mental and spiritual blindness. After decades of captivity in Babylon, they were back in Jerusalem with an opportunity to rebuild their city and their lives, yet they languished and could not see why things were not going well. Remind the group of the concepts of situational blindness and situational awareness, and apply these to God's people at this time. Then ask: Have you ever faced circumstances so overwhelming or discouraging that you experienced "situational blindness"? What happened? How did you "regain your vision" and move ahead?

Enter the Bible Story

Ask a volunteer to read aloud Zechariah 7:9-14. Then remind the group about the conditions in Jerusalem to which the people returned following their Babylonian exile. The Temple had been destroyed and looted; most of the city was in ruins; the city's protective wall was in shambles; the population was smaller than before; resources were scarce. Even though the people were "home," they were still living under foreign domination. Other people had, during their exile, settled in the area and laid claim to parts of the territory. Worship had been compromised by the influence of pagan cults. Though the people had been sanctioned to rebuild the Temple, they got only so far as rebuilding the altar and repairing the foundation. Their focus was on rebuilding houses for themselves. They had become spiritually blind.

Using information in "The Men and the Mission" and "Prophetic Reality Check," identify the prophets Haggai and Zephaniah and their tasks as prophets to God's people. Ask group members to refer to these sections and to the writings of the prophet Haggai and respond to these questions: What excuses did the people give for not rebuilding the Temple? What did they focus on instead? What struggles did they face? How did this affect their relationship with God?

Note Haggai's repeated refrains to the people to "take your ways to heart" (Haggai 1:5, 7) and "take it to heart" (2:15, 18). Ask group members to suggest what this means and why it can be unpleasant. The section "Taking Our Ways to Heart" provides some concise statements about what the prophets tell us about living with situational awareness. Review and discuss these statements as a group. Then ask: Have you ever had to face an unpleasant truth about yourself? What caused you to "take your ways to heart?"

Live the Story

Recall for the group the information about Thomas Lowes and the inscription in his memory at The Palace of Holyroodhouse in Edinburgh, Scotland. Read aloud part of the inscription, connecting it both to God's people at the time of Haggai and Zechariah and to God's people today. Then read aloud the Faith Focus Statement for this session: God's people are defined not by political or military power nor by prosperity or by poverty. God's children are known by proper worship and covenant living.

Ask group members to respond silently to these questions: How do you define yourself? What role do your accomplishments, possessions, and position play in how you see yourself? Will your investments of time, energy, and other resources last beyond your lifetime? What are the only sure and eternal things in which we can invest? How do we do this?

Close with a prayer, asking God to eliminate situational blindness and give you clear vision for who you are and how you are to live as God's people. Ask God to help you let go of the past and move ahead into the future God has prepared for you. Commit to take God's ways to heart and choose God's purposes over your own.

6. Haggai and Zechariah: Profound Possibilities
Haggai and Zechariah

Faith Focus
We can have faith in God's ultimate plan for us without understanding all the details. It is enough to know that God always has the last word.

Before the Session
Search online for the stories behind how certain things came to be invented. In your search, use key words such as "stories behind practical inventions." Select a couple of examples to share as a way to introduce the concept of seeing new possibilities.

Think of a time in your life when you had a profound "Aha!" moment and be prepared to talk about this experience with your group.

Obtain votive candles, enough for each person in your group to have one; a long, flat baking dish, at least two inches deep; and matches. Before the group arrives, fill the baking dish with water at least an inch deep.

Claim Your Story
Begin by explaining how a few common items came to be invented. For example, Joseph Friedman invented the flexible drinking straw in the 1930s after watching his young daughter struggle to drink a milkshake out of a straight paper straw. Using a screw and some dental floss, he created corrugations in the straight straw so that it bent over the edge of the glass and made it easier for his daughter and future generations of small children to drink.[2]

Next, ask group members to recall times in their lives when they had an "Aha!" moment. What were the circumstances? What caused them to see things in a new light? How did things change for them after that? Encourage them to tell their own stories by sharing a similar experience you have had.

Recall for the group the illustration of the "diverging diamond" traffic pattern and how it illustrates a combination of imagination and engineering—in the eyes of the Walt Disney Company, "Imagineering." Ask if anyone can think of other examples of this concept. Then note that rather than "Imagineering," Haggai and Zechariah challenge us to employ faith to see things in a new light, from God's point of view. When we do, we, like the people of God to whom they first spoke, become aware of great new possibilities.

Enter the Bible Story
Offer a brief summary of what we know about the prophets Haggai and Zechariah, the times and circumstances during which they lived and ministered,

and their concerns and messages. Encourage group members to offer details based on their readings and recollections.

Write on the board the following words and phrases: "the Lord of Heavenly Forces," "the Temple," "faithfulness/unfaithfulness," "God's purposes," "repentance," "the Law," "vision/the big picture," "insight," "hope." Ask the group to explain the significance of each to the work of Haggai and Zechariah and to the people of God at this point in their history. Refer to the section "The Lord of Heavenly Forces," as necessary. Use the writer's illustration of the Sanibel Stoop to remind the group of the importance of avoiding a narrow focus and instead looking up and away in order to have a better vision of God's purposes for us and for the world.

Reinforce the importance of the Law, the Temple, and vision for the community of faith. Then, one by one, briefly review Zechariah's visions and what they meant, reading portions of the biblical text aloud, as time permits. Note how the visions progressively reveal God's plans for Israel. Then ask: What set the stage for the people's return to Jerusalem? What was God prepared to do?

Explain why Zechariah 9-14 has sometimes been called Second Zechariah and what the prophecies in these chapters reflect. Review particularly the actions in Chapter 9. Then ask: What did the prophet say must occur before complete renewal could happen? Refer the group to Chapter 11 and briefly explain its symbolism.

Using the information in "Zechariah's Day of the Lord," review the last three chapters of Zechariah, reading aloud key verses from his prophecies that speak of assurance, renewal, redemption, and peace. Ask: What must the people do in order to experience peace? What qualities must permeate their lives?

Point out that although the remnant of God's people in Jerusalem was small, God nonetheless chose to dwell in their midst. God forgave their sin and promised to bring new life and peace to Jerusalem. Ask a volunteer to read aloud Zechariah 8:8 and stress that this is God's promise to us, too.

Live the Story

Acknowledge, as the writer does, that fear rather than strength often characterizes our response to life and its circumstances. Personal sin, uncertainty, doubt, worry, grief, misplaced priorities, and many other things darken our vision for what God is doing within and around us.

Recall the illustration and comments of Michael Arad, who designed the 9/11 memorial at the site of the World Trade Center in New York City. Read aloud the last paragraph of "Live the Story" (page 67). Give each person a votive candle and ask them to place it in the dish of water and light it. Ask each person to think of both a personal and a corporate/global concern that threatens to block their vision of God's bigger picture. Ask each to pray silently for God to replace fear with faith in and hope for total redemption and renewal. Then close with a voiced prayer such as this:

God of redemption and renewal, we confess that we are sometimes more fearful than faithful. We allow circumstances to block our vision of who you are and what you are doing in us and in the world. Help us to look beyond what we can see with our limited vision and touch with our hands. Open us to new and profound possibilities. Shine your light of hope within us, and use us to reflect your hope to those who still walk in darkness and fear. Give us the courage to live into your ultimate plan for us, even when we don't know or understand all the details. Remind us that it is enough to know that you always have the last word. Amen.

7. Malachi: Calling for a Spiritual Makeover
Malachi

Faith Focus
God remains faithful even when we do not. Even when we stray, God's invitation remains: Return to me.

Before the Session
Write the word "people" on several small cards or paper strips; write the word "priests" on several other cards or paper strips. Prepare enough cards or paper strips for everyone in your group to have one.

From construction paper, cut strips approximately 1½ inches by 11 inches. Cut enough paper strips for everyone in your group to have two or three. Also cut some extras to have on hand.

Gather paper and pens or pencils for making notes, and glue sticks or tape.

Claim Your Story
Begin by asking group members to identify and describe reality shows they watch or are familiar with. Guide the conversation to focus particularly on shows within this genre that seek to catch people unaware, as the writer has done on pages 69–70. Then ask: Have you ever been observed without your knowledge, only to learn later that the individual(s) who saw and/or heard you came away with less than positive conclusions about you and your character? What were the circumstances? Were you able to resolve the situation?

The writer mentions reality "makeover" shows and notes that prophets like Malachi are helpful to us when we need a spiritual makeover. Ask: Have you ever considered a "spiritual makeover"? What would this consist of? How would you go about it?

Enter the Bible Story
Briefly introduce the prophet Malachi, whose name in Hebrew means "my messenger." Describe the circumstances during which he ministered. Although the Temple had been rebuilt and rededicated, the people of God, including the priests, were not living faithfully within the covenant. Point out some of the examples of their faithlessness that the writer mentions on pages 70–71.

Remind the group that Malachi's prophecy consists of six disputes that let the people and the priests know that God had been observing them. Ask a volunteer to read aloud Malachi 1:1-5, the first dispute. Briefly explain Malachi's point and what he said God would do. Then ask: Have you ever you questioned God's faithfulness? What caused you to do that? What can we do to correct ourselves when we question God's faithfulness?

Lead the group to examine the remaining five disputes. Divide into two groups by giving each person a card with either the word "people" or the word "priests" written on it. Ask them to scan the book of Malachi and make a list of the charges against either the people or the priests. Provide paper and pens or pencils. Suggest that they jot down key words or phrases and cite the chapter and verse references to use later in describing the issues more fully. Refer them to the section "Arguing With God" for additional information. After several minutes, reassemble the group and guide them in summarizing what they discovered by asking questions such as these:

- What were the people and the priests guilty of in terms of the offerings they made to God? What did their offerings reflect in terms of their trust in God?
- What was God's response to their offerings?
- What did Malachi say would happen to the priests who had disgraced their holy calling?
- What had the people begun to do that resulted in polluting the worship of God?
- How had the people forsaken their covenant responsibilities?
- What had the people accused God of doing?
- What did Malachi challenge the people to do?

Return to the idea of a spiritual makeover and acknowledge that this is what Malachi called God's people to pursue. Lead the group to consider personal spiritual makeovers by connecting some of their experiences to those of God's people during Malachi's time. Ask them to ponder silently the answers to the following questions and statements. Pause briefly after you read each one aloud.

- In what specific circumstances have you failed to trust God to meet your needs? Confess that to God now, and place your trust in God to always take care of you.
- When have you found worship and other spiritual disciplines tedious or meaningless? Ask God to renew God's spirit within you and restore the joy of your salvation. Commit to approaching prayer, worship, Bible study, and other spiritual disciplines with pure motives and a clean heart.
- What have you placed ahead of your allegiance to God? What is more important to you than God? Ask God to forgive you.
- Have you ever questioned God's integrity or God's intentions? Acknowledge to God that God, rather than you, knows what is best and is working to achieve his ultimate purposes.
- When have you experienced God's patience and forgiveness, in spite of your fickleness and backsliding? Thank God for these gifts.

• Have obedience, faithfulness, and service to God ever seemed useless or a waste of time to you? Have you ever doubted God's love for you? Be assured that God loves you, knows about your faithfulness and service, and rewards righteous living. Thank God for this blessing.

Remind the group that Malachi's prophecy, and the Old Testament, end with words of both warning and hope. Read aloud Malachi 4:1-6. Stress that Malachi was fully confident of God's goodness toward those who love and serve him. He firmly believed that what we say and do makes a difference. The choice in how we live in relation to God is ours. God's invitation to us, even when we stray, is "Return to me."

Live the Story
Read aloud the second paragraph of "Live the Story" on page 76. Give everyone two or three construction paper strips and ask them to identify some of the "old chains" they have dragged around, such as unbelief, pride, arrogance, greed, idolatry, and injustice. Encourage them to identify others as well. Ask them to write these on paper strips. Connect the strips to make a paper chain. Ask the group to stand and form a circle, and place the paper chain on the floor in the middle of the circle. Then read aloud the last paragraph of "Live the Story" on pages 76–77.

Close with a prayer asking God to remove the chains that keep you from fully returning to and serving him faithfully. Commit to God your very best. Thank God for life and the blessing of living it in relation to God.

8. The Minor Prophets:
Information, Inspiration, Blessing, and Change
Micah—Malachi

Faith Focus
Prophetic information and inspiration keep us "growing up" into the people God created us to be.

Before the Session
On a large poster or piece of paper, duplicate the chart found in "Enter the Bible Story" below. Obtain several markers.

Copy the verses from "Live the Story," pages 87–88, onto separate strips of posterboard or heavy paper. You may want to prepare one for each person in your group and laminate them, making bookmarks.

Claim Your Story
Remind the group about George Washington Carver, using the information on pages 79–80. Read aloud the quotation attributed to him: "Inspiration is never at variance with information. In fact, the more information one has, the greater

will be the inspiration." Connect this thought with the inspiration and information the ancient people of God—and we—get from the Minor Prophets. Ask the group to consider and summarize some key things they have learned from your study of the Minor Prophets. What has been most surprising? What has been most challenging?

Enter the Bible Story

Remind the group about the period of time and the circumstances during which Micah, Nahum, Habakkuk, Zephaniah, Haggai, Zechariah, and Malachi ministered. Ask each person in the group, in round-robin fashion, to suggest one word to summarize the prophets' overall message. Encourage each person to come up with a different descriptive word. Select a few ahead of time to have in mind and offer them first, if necessary. Some possibilities include: judgment, warning, promise, faithfulness, hope, redemption. Affirm all responses, and remind the group that while the prophets did offer stern warnings and tell of horrible consequences of the people's disobedience and sin, they always offered hope and extended the possibility of redemption and salvation. For them and for us, the final word is always *hope.*

Next, ask the group to suggest some qualities of God's character we learn about from these prophets. Ask them to recall specific examples from this study. How would you characterize God based on the messages of the prophets? What kind of god is our God? What does God expect from us? How do we know?

Note the great degree to which the Minor Prophets are a major presence in the New Testament. Spend some time reviewing texts from Micah, Zephaniah, Malachi, and Zechariah that point to the birth, ministry, and passion of Jesus (see page 82). Ask volunteers to read aloud the prophetic text, followed by the Gospel text, and identify the truth to which each points.

Next, call attention to the chart on page 110, which you have duplicated on a poster or large piece of paper. Lay this on a flat surface where it is accessible to everyone, and distribute markers. Explain that the center column contains phrases related to teachings of Jesus to which we find references both in the prophetic writings and in the New Testament. Guide your group to do a Scripture search to locate both the prophetic and the New Testament references to each teaching and to summarize the teaching and fill in the chart. Depending upon the size of your group, you can assign one or two teachings to each person, or you can divide the teachings among small groups. Or, you may want to divide into two groups, one for Prophets and the other for New Testament, and ask each group to locate the specific references. (Specific chapters and verses can be found in the section "Teaching of Jesus," pages 82–83.) Allow the group plenty of time to conduct their search, and spend a few minutes talking about each teaching of Jesus and what it means for us.

Remind the group what the prophets meant by references to the "day of judgment." Select verses from both the prophets and the New Testament and ask volunteers to read them aloud to summarize key biblical teachings about this important theme (see "Day of Judgment and Salvation," page 83).

Prophet	Teaching of Jesus	New Testament
Micah	Justice and mercy toward others; humility and love toward God	Matthew Mark
Haggai	What is holy	Matthew
Zechariah	Jesus: humble and gentle King	Matthew John
Zechariah	Jesus' blood of the covenant	Matthew
Zechariah	Jesus, the Good Shepherd	John
Zechariah	Cleansing and saving water of life	John Revelation
Zechariah	Merchants in God's house	John
Malachi	Corrupt leaders who burden God's people	Matthew
Malachi	John the Baptist	Matthew Mark Luke
Malachi	John/Elijah	Matthew Luke

Finally, note specific examples from Paul's writings that demonstrate how familiar he was with the prophets and the degree to which their writings influenced him. The section "Teaching of Paul," pages 84–85, highlights several of these.

The writer stresses the connection between information and inspiration and the changes these can and should bring in our lives. Point out the three examples of hopeful change from the New Testament. Then lead the group to consider how they have been challenged to change their lives as a result of information and inspiration, particularly during this study. Ask questions such as these: Because of new insights into the character of God you have gained from the information and inspiration of the prophets, how do you see yourself differently? How do you think God sees you? How is God calling you to change as a result of this new information and inspiration? Who are you to become as a result of what you now know? On a scale of 1–10, how would you rate your willingness to change, with 1 being "not very open" and 10 being "completely open"?

Live the Story

Distribute the verses from the prophets that you copied onto individual strips of posterboard or paper. Ask volunteers to read these aloud. Then read aloud the final paragraph of "Live the Story," page 89. Close with this prayer, or one of your own.

Creator and Creating God, we thank you that your work with us is not finished. We acknowledge that we have a long way to go toward becoming the people you created us to be. Because of our sin, we move farther away from that goal rather than closer to it some days. We thank you for reminders from the prophets, the Gospel writers, from Paul, and from Jesus that both challenge and encourage us to not lose sight of who you have called us to become. Help us continue to learn and grow in knowledge of you and your ways. And may that knowledge bring in us the changes you desire to see. Give us hope for the journey, and guide us as we go. In the name of the one who walked before us and walks beside us and within us. Amen.

1. From *http://www.brainyquote.com/quotes/authors/h/helen_keller.html.*
2. From *http://invention.smithsonian.org/resources/online_articles_detail.aspx?id=301.*

IMMERSE YOURSELF IN ANOTHER VOLUME

IMMERSION
Bible Studies

Available at Cokesbury and other booksellers　　　　AbingdonPress.com

BKM126600001 PACP01238834-01